The 2011 Money Saver's Guide

By: D. Richard Davis

All Rights reserved. No part of this book may be used or reproduced in any manner whatsoever without written permission of the publisher

Produced by D. Richard Davis
Designed by Judy Spencer
ISBN-13: 978-1456399726
ISBN-10: 1456399721

Copyright 2010 D. Richard Davis

Contents

Your Money Makeover	3
Real Estate	32
The Psychology of Saving Money	57
Understanding the World of Finance	66
Taxes, Retirement, and College	83
Automobile Expenses	97
Technology and Saving Money	105

"A penny saved is a penny earned," is an adage that we have all heard. I disagree with that statement. A penny saved is better than a penny earned. You don't pay tax on money that you save, whereas taxes can take up nearly 50 percent of your income, depending on your tax bracket.

If you were to save 70 percent on a new water heater, you are also saving on 70 percent of the sales tax you would have paid, 70 percent of the income tax on money that was not spent, and any extra finance charges you avoid; as well as the original 70 percent off of the retail price. When you take into account all of the other taxes and fees associated with the money we spend, the rewards of saving money become exponentially greater.

In this book, we are going to cover thousands of ways that you can save money. But remember, that the simple act of saving money is not the ultimate goal. I want to teach you to live better: find higher quality goods and services, manage time and resources so we can spend more on things we like to do, live healthier, and reach higher goals in your careers and family lives.

I want you to not focus on just the dollars and cents you can save, but to live by the economic concept of maximizing utility. Utility is an economic term signifying the ability of a good or service to satisfy the needs or wants of a consumer. Our resources are limited, or in other words, we only have a certain amount of money to pay for the things that we need and want. Our spending habits should not be based on dollar amounts, but instead we should focus on getting more needs or wants satisfied.

The end result is living well. I want you to live and feel like kings and queens, while staying within the limited budget that one's income would require. That being said, you are also going to find strategies that will significantly increase your bottom line.

Using This Book

This book is organized in a way to use your time more efficiently. The first section of this book is called "Your Money Makeover", and is broken into specific spending categories of your everyday lives where money can be saved. I would encourage you to read this section one of two ways: You can read page-by-page like any other book and internalize the concepts that are going to positively affect your life and habits, or you can each day pick one section, one page, or one paragraph and seriously ponder it so that you can figure out how you can utilize it. After all, the greatest concepts are useless without any action on your part.

      Many of my clients like to hold family meetings once a week where they discuss sections from this book together. Not only is it an effective way for everyone to get ideas out on the table, but it will also galvanize an entire family towards reaching a healthy goal. You can trim down your household expenses while at that same time bringing your family together. That is living well. *That is maximizing utility.*

      There are sections later in the book that go into further detail on complex money-saving tips. The real estate chapter, for example, covers in finer detail the many intricacies of real estate spending and how you can plan and save large sums of money over a long period of time. These sections are just as important but will take longer and more focus to cover.

Setting Goals

As you read, don't just look for good tips on saving money, but set goals for yourself on how you are going to use them. I would recommend having a small notebook to jot your ideas on as you read. Draw a line through the middle of the page so on the left side you can write the concept or tip you have learned, and on the right side you can write the corresponding ideas you have for implementing that tip in your life.

Set some concrete goals and resolutions for the year of 2011. How much money would you like to save? How can you make your family finances more stable? The news media can't decide whether we are out of a recession or not, but you can choose to end your individual recession right now. Make the choice. Cultivate good habits now.

The only way our leaders and country as a whole can become better and balance our national budget is by individuals like you taking responsibility and making good financial decisions. You will be able to better your own life as well as those around you. You can be the change that we want to see in the world.

Money Makeover

As I previously stated, the next portion is going to be organized into categories of spending in our lives. Each paragraph is a tip that will help you to curb spending and maximize the benefits that you receive from your money spent. Please consider real-life applications with every tip that you read. Good luck!

Everyday & Lifestyle Spending

Exercise for Less: If you're just staying in shape and not training for a Strongman competition, you can drop the gym membership. This will save you as much as $360 a year. Unless you're training for competition, a gym can be expensive overkill. You can buy cheap weights at yard sales or places like Play It Again Sports. Better yet, find them free at sites like craigslist or Freecycle. You can buy cheap workout videos and exercise in front of the TV, or get both exercise and fresh air by walking, jogging or biking in your neighborhood. You can bike to work and save in transportation costs.

Limit Your Clothing Spending: I will often ask my clients to set a specific dollar amount—say $40—and they will not spend more than that on any article of clothing. Some people cannot live without their designer items, and I wouldn't dare tell them they need to stop buying them. But if you are on a tighter budget than usual, you can still get new fashions and look good for much less. Stores such as H&M, Forever 21, and Old Navy make it easy to buy cheap, stylish clothing. While you'll probably need to make some exceptions, such as for a winter jacket, the vast majority of your wardrobe can be purchased on the cheap.

Don't Skimp on Everything: Sometimes trying to save money can actually whisk more cash from your pocket. When you have to replace something because it wears out too quickly or doesn't do the job, a great bargain can turn into a raw deal. Items like a good men's suit or dress shoes can last a long time if they are high quality-- and there are career benefits to dressing sharply. Also, furniture that is more durable may cost a bit more but will be cost efficient in the long run.

Eat In on Vacation: Book a suite with a kitchen at an extended-stay hotel, which charges on average from $30 to $100 per night. Even if you have to pay a bit more for the accommodations, you'll easily save money by not taking your family out for breakfast ($5 a person), lunch ($10), and dinner ($15). After the cost of groceries, this could save you $70 a day with a family of four.

Use Your Calendar: Whenever you rent something - library books, videos, etc. – mark it on your calendar and save money by avoiding those quickly mounting late fees. Many stores and libraries also now offer email reminders to help the constantly harried so sign up for the extra help. You wouldn't believe what some households pay in late fees to the video store.

Avoid Window Shopping: We all have our weak spots, like home goods, electronics or clothes -- even if you don't like to go to the mall. You don't even have to leave the house to window shop anymore; those catalogs, the internet and commercials advertising the latest sale can be just as tempting. Window shopping is a bad financial habit that takes some discipline to break. Staying away from stores and not requesting catalogs or email updates from your favorite stores is a good place to start. Before buying that latest item you pine for, ask yourself two questions: Do I need it and can I pay cash for it? If your answer is no, walk away.

Don't Carry a Lot of Cash: Charging on a card can be a bad thing if you're not able to pay it off, but carrying lots of cash can be just as bad a habit. Cash can give you the feeling of having extra – cash that is "burning a hole in your pocket." Only carry enough cash for what you need, and leave the rest at home. Avoiding plastic is great, but budgeting is just as important when choosing to pay cash. If you like the green, try budgeting your cash with envelopes: one for groceries, one for entertainment, etc.

Sell Things You Don't Need: If you're like most people, you've got clothes you don't wear, CDs you don't listen to, books you don't read, DVDs you don't watch, furniture you don't sit in – you get the picture. Take it to a consignment shop or a swap meet; sell it online at eBay or craigslist; have a yard sale. If nothing else, donate it and create a tax deduction. But don't mess up your quality of life by stressing out and trying to do everything at once. Pick one thing (or room) every month of 2011, clear out the clutter and make some extra money.

Uncouple Your Emotions and Spending Habits: It was a rough week, or a good one, or you want to reward yourself for losing a few pounds, so you go shopping. You earned that new dress, that new gadget, that big pie – it was on sale, too. Letting your mood dictate your buying decisions is a road to financial ruin. Sober up before shopping. Do you need these items, and can you afford them? Be honest with yourself. Reward yourself by doing something that doesn't cost, like taking a nice bath, or spending time with your loved ones.

Learn to Haggle: It never hurts to ask if prices can be lowered and the potential savings here are sky-high. According to this survey by Consumer Reports, negotiating a lower price is not only possible, it's likely. What can you negotiate? Pretty much everything. Even department stores offer some type of discount if you push the right buttons. You can call your credit card company and ask for a better interest rate. You can ask for a lower price from your doctor. You can negotiate a lower price on your cable bill. The fact is, you can negotiate a lower price on anything from home electronics to hotel rooms.

Capitalize on Your Privileges: Are you an AAA member? Do you belong to the AARP? What about your local credit union? Check organizations you have memberships with to see if they offer buying privileges or discounts. When flying, staying in hotels, or renting cars, sign up for their loyalty programs for discounts and extra freebies.

Coupons Instead of Gifts: As you plan your holiday shopping, consider this: Giving the gift of your time in the form of a coupon to take your mom to a museum, or out for tea, can be far more meaningful than buying her a cashmere sweater. In my family, this has been a long-standing tradition that has brought us closer together. I would much rather receive one of these coupons from my kids than another necktie on Christmas!

Go Cold Turkey: Smoking, overeating and drinking are costly habits to maintain. Kicking the habit is a hard thing to do, and many enjoy their little vices. But you can save boatloads of money getting them out of your life. You'll save money by cutting out on the regular spending it's costing you, and you'll probably save on insurance premiums and long-term health costs. It's the ultimate win-win.

Around the House

Paint Your Roof White: I'm just going to throw this one out there because it is definitely not for everyone. A recent study found that in sunny climates, buildings with white roofs required up to 40 percent less energy for cooling than those with black roofs. At current utility rates, that means you could save $150 or more per year in cooling costs. If you have a paint airbrush/roller or know a friend with one, you could get the paint for 1/4 of the yearly savings and all it would cost you is a Saturday afternoon. The downside: your roof is white. I'm sure it fits some homes better than others.

Upgrade Your Appliances: Many state and local governments and utility companies offer financial incentives for homeowners to upgrade their appliances to newer, more energy-efficient models. These incentives usually take the form of rebate checks for homeowners who can provide proof of purchase. In the state of New York there are 47 separate tax incentives, grants and rebate programs. That includes a state program that offers a rebate of $105 for an energy-efficient refrigerator if you recycle the old one, $75 for a freezer and $100 for a clothes washer.

Smart Landscaping: Landscaping with the right mix of trees and shrubs can lower your energy bills by blocking winter wind and summer sun. There are many books available about efficient landscaping ideas. You can also focus on plants that are extra-efficient in their water usage to lower your watering costs.

Only Renovate If You'll Get a Return: Renovating your kitchen at a national average cost of about $43,860 doesn't always mean you'll make it back when you sell your house. In fact, you'll probably recoup only 91 percent, or $39,920, according to a 2009 study. On average, you'll recover 85 percent of the cost of a new roof ($9,460 of $11,160) and 90 percent of the cost of new windows ($8,680 of $9,680). A bathroom renovation is the project least likely to lose money (a return of $10,730 on the average cost of $10,500, or 102 percent). A wiser option is hiring a professional who can give your home an inexpensive makeover—known as "staging". Ask your real estate agent for contact info on some local staging experts and you can boost your selling price with little investment.

Be Careful With Pet Care: Consider alternative ways to get health care for your pet. Humane society or university veterinary clinics may offer thriftier medical services than private practitioners. And always seek a second opinion when a vet suggests a pricey procedure. If you thought that healthcare for humans was mismanaged, you would be surprised how much variation there is in pet healthcare prices between practices. You should always shop around.

Reconsider Getting a Pet: I know I say this at the risk of offending half of my readers, so don't take this the wrong way—It is just something to consider. Sure it sounds heartless, but did you realize that welcoming home a puppy can cost you an average of more than $1,500 a year - or $15,000 over 10 years? Cats are expensive too - just under $1,000 a year or approximately $9,000 for 10 years of care. Looking at the long-term picture, that's a new car or the down payment on a home. Keep walking right past that pet store and keep the money in your pocket instead.

Save Money on Expensive Tools: You can save a lot of money by asking to borrow or rent household items from neighbors. Ask your local neighborhood association whether they have a tool-lending system set up. If they don't, you should try to set one up with neighbors you know. You can easily set up a Google Docs spreadsheet online that can be edited by all users and ask your neighbors to add in the inventory of their toolbox. You can also save a lot of money by renting instead of buying equipment that will not be used frequently.

Utility Bills

Energy Sweeps at Night: We all have left fans, lights or appliances on at night while we sleep, but doing so wastes increasingly expensive energy. To save money, do a nightly sweep through the house to make sure all your electric devices are turned off before you go to bed. It may be a pain, but the savings from simply turning everything off can add up quickly. It takes about $9 per year to run just one compact fluorescent light bulb through the night, $21 for a conventional bulb and $35 for a big ceiling fan on high. Over a year, this can add up to some big savings.

Smart Thermostats: If you don't have one now, a programmable thermostat can play this role for your home automatically. Based on your family's schedule, you can program it to automatically set the target temperature higher in the summer and lower in the winter when your family won't be home. Prices on the thermostats have come down so much – you can buy one at a hardware store for as little as $25 – that installing one is a no-brainer, especially because the EPA estimates the average homeowner can save $180 per year with a properly programmed unit.

Setting Your Water Heater: Not only does heating your water too hot create the danger of scalding, it can cost you cash. The Environmental Protection Agency estimates that a heater set at 140 degrees or higher can waste $36 to $61 annually in standby heat losses to keep water at that temperature, and more than $400 to bring fresh water up to that high temperature. To save even more money, you can turn your electric heater off or turn your gas heater down when you go on vacation to save even more. Keeping it at 120 degrees when you are home should be sufficient, while staying efficient.

Install an Irrigation Meter: I'm going to tell you something that many people don't know. Do you know that you are charged twice for the water you use every month – once to pump it into your house and again to pump it out as sewage? The assumption is every gallon of water that you run out of your faucet is going to go back down the drain. But if you use water to irrigate your lawn or garden, that water never makes it into the sewer system, thus, you should not be charged sewage expenses for those many gallons. To save money by making sure you're only paying for the sewer capacity you're using, many utilities offer the option to get a separate meter to measure water usage for irrigation, swimming pools and other outdoor uses.

Look for the Energy Star: Energy Star is a government subsidized program that identifies energy-efficient products, especially as it relates to energy-intensive items like water heaters and clothes dryers. But Energy Star labels won't just help you save money on big, expensive appliances. Energy Star rates all kinds of items like light bulbs, TVs, clothes washers, refrigerators, furnaces, fans, and more And while an Energy Star light bulb won't yield as much savings as an Energy Star refrigerator, those savings do add up. Even if the items are prices higher, you can rest assured you will recoup your investment. The EPA won't grant the Energy Star label unless its figures show you'll recoup that extra outlay within five years or less on electricity and water costs.

Reusable Filters: Waiting a long time to change your filter makes your HVAC system less efficient and costs you more in electricity. Dirt and neglect can even cause your expensive HVAC unit to die an untimely death. But how many times have you put off switching filters because you didn't have a fresh one on hand. You should get reusable filters. Using a permanent filter, you'll save money in the long run, cut your utility bill and prolong the life of your HVAC unit. If the disposable AC filters that must be changed every three months are around $4 each, you can recoup the $20 to $40 cost of a permanent filter in as little as 15 months.

Seal Up Your Home: When you add up the cumulative effect of all the small leaks in your home, it has the effect of leaving a window open all year long. To save money, you can use inexpensive expanding foam or caulk available at your local hardware store to seal cracks in the following areas where cold or warm air typically escapes. Those places include: around windows and doorframes, around the top of the basement wall where the cement or block contacts the wooden frame, known as the rim joist, and around the holes in walls where pipes enter and exit your home.

Stop Wasted Water Usage: Turn off the tap while you're brushing your teeth or shaving—every minute the water flows wastes up to 2½ gallons, according to the Environmental Protection Agency. Run full loads in washing machines and dishwashers. Water plants in the early morning to ensure that the water goes into the ground instead of evaporating. And use a bucket to wash the car, hosing it off for a quick rinse, to save 90 gallons of water per wash. This can add up to a savings of $190 a year for an average size household.

Make Sure Your Bill and Meter Match Up: Utility workers make mistakes just like the rest of us, and when they make mistakes reading your meter, it can be costly. While you'll probably notice a big error on your utility bill, you may not catch more subtle errors. Make sure you're only getting charged for the electricity you actually used by comparing the meter reading on your utility bill to what you actually see on your meter. If the amount on your meter is lower than the one on your bill, that's a dead giveaway that you're being overcharged.

Other Bills

Stop Sending Bills By Mail: The average household receives about 15 bills a month. With stamps now at 44 cents each, you spend about $79 a year just on postage—and don't forget the late fees if your checks get lost in the mail. Save time and money by signing up with the billers' customer-service departments to have your bills paid by credit card or automatic debit; payments will be documented on your monthly bank statement. If you want more control, almost all major banks offer free online bill payment, which lets you schedule payments in advance.

Lose Cell Phone Charges That You Don't Need: Too many minutes and you're wasting money. Too few and the overages can skyrocket your cell-phone bill. On average, according to the consumer research firm J.D. Power & Associates, cell-phone subscribers use only 64 percent of the minutes they pay for. If you're still under contract, call your cell-phone company and ask it to analyze your usage. You may find that buying fewer monthly minutes but, say, getting unlimited evening and weekend minutes may work better than a more expensive plan—and you won't pay a termination fee of $100 or more. If your contract is up and you're thinking about switching carriers, carefully consider what will fit your usage best after analyzing your usage.

Bundle Your Services: Consider a package deal from your local cable or phone company. You can get digital phone service, which is provided by a broadband Internet connection, high-speed Internet, and digital channels for much less than you'd pay separately. For example, Comcast currently offers all three services for $115 a month in the Northeast (price varies by region), a 33 percent savings over the à la carte price. Start by shopping for Internet access at BuyTelco (buytelco.net); then ask local providers what deals they offer when you bundle with phone and TV service.

Don't Use Cash to Pay Tolls: Sign up for an electronic toll device, such as E-ZPass (ezpass.com), which is now good on a number of toll roads, bridges, and tunnels in 13 states from Illinois to Maine; FasTrak in California; SunPass in Florida; or PikePass in Oklahoma. You'll save time and fuel by not idling in toll lanes, and some toll roads offer regular commuters discounts of as much as 50 percent. The International Bridge, Tunnel, and Turnpike Association (ibtta.org) lists websites for local toll authorities and their discount details.

Manage Your Landline: Every few months, comparison shop to see if you're paying too much for your telecommunications services – Internet, land line phone and cable/satellite service. Many times, competing companies will offer better deals to new customers. If you find a better deal, contact your telecom providers and negotiate – or switch. You should cancel all the

extra services you don't use, such as call waiting, caller ID, voicemail, call forwarding and three-way calling.
Look Into VoIP: Switching to an Internet telephone service, sometimes called Voice over IP, or VoIP, can save you big, especially if you make a lot of long-distance or international calls. VoIP providers often charge only a flat fee and don't have all the tacked-on taxes and fees that traditional telephone services do. Vonage (Vonage.com) even recently came out with an unlimited long distance plan that costs only $15 a month with no contract required. This could cut most consumers' phone bills in half.

Home Finances

Take Advantage of Flexible Spending Accounts: Employers offer flexible-spending accounts that let you sock away up to $5,000 per household tax-free for medical expenses, which you can use for health-insurance copayments, prescription drugs, eyeglasses, contact lenses, and even nonprescription drugs, such as aspirin. Estimate your needs carefully when open enrollment comes along. The IRS now offers a grace period of an extra 2½ months to spend the money, so you don't have to rush to spend it all by the end of the calendar year. You can also set up transportation-reimbursement accounts to save money on parking fees and bus and train fares—$2,460 for parking or $1,260 for transit. Just save your receipts and fax or mail them in with the required form and you'll get a check in the mail or have the reimbursement deposited into your bank account.
Get Rid of Mortgage Insurance: Make extra mortgage payments, whether monthly, once a year or on some other schedule, to get to 80 percent LTV (loan-to-value ratio) and cancel your private mortgage insurance (PMI) more quickly. One way for those on a 26-pay-per-year salary schedule is to make an extra mortgage payment in months where you get three paychecks instead of two. Remember that if you have already reached your 80 percent LTV you can cancel your PMI right away.

Don't Over-Insure: Get a hold of your agent or a trusted expert and review your insurance policies. Does your home owner's insurance include the value of the land, for example? The land isn't going anywhere, even in a twister, so you don't need to insure it—just the structure and your belongings. If you have an older car, the annual premiums and deductible might make collision and comprehensive insurance cost more than the car is worth. On any insurance policy, auto or home, think about a higher deductible. Because filing numerous small claims can raise your insurance rates, you may be better off covering minor losses yourself and getting a lower rate with a high-deductible policy. You may also have unneeded special riders on high-value items you no longer own.

No More Bounced Checks: Sign up for overdraft protection and link a savings account, credit card, or line of credit to your checking account. Almost all banks offer this service for free or for a nominal annual fee of $5, and they typically charge $3 to $5 per transfer. You're responsible only for paying the interest on any credit you use, and you can avoid that by using the money in your savings account as your backup.

Don't Pay For Credit Reports: The Web abounds with ads for free credit reports, but many sites try to get you to pay extra for fancier reports. Federal law entitles you to a free credit report from each of the three major bureaus, Equifax, Experian, and TransUnion (annualcreditreport.com). One thing to be aware of: A credit report will show your payment history and any identity-theft activity, but it doesn't include the credit score. Rest assured, as long as you are making sure your credit report is free of damaging data, the credit score will be on track. We will discuss maintaining a high credit score later in the book.

Invest Your Emergency Money: Personal finance gurus often exhort you to save six month's salary away—just in case. This is great advice, but many are tucking this all away in a savings account. I advise my clients to store two months' salary into a savings account and invest the rest. Otherwise, you lose out on the interest that extra four months' salary could be earning in a CD or a money-market fund, or you're wasting money paying finance charges on credit-card balances you could be whittling down. For an unexpected expenditure, a home-equity line of credit, which usually costs nothing until you use it, can be tapped in an emergency.

Get Credit Cards with No Annual Fee: Frequent-flier cards make sense only if you charge $10,000 or more annually. For most people who pay off balances monthly or don't charge much, a no-annual-fee cash-back card, such as the Citi CashReturns MasterCard (citibank.com) or the Chase Freedom Credit Card (chase.com), is a wise bet. Both offer cash back, ranging from 1 percent to 3 percent, on purchases (standard maximum rebate is $300 a year). Other cards may have a higher maximum cash-back reward, but you have to spend more or follow complex rules to earn it. If you carry a balance, forget reward or cash-back cards altogether and opt for a card with a lower interest rate. Switching from a cash-back card with a 17 percent rate to a no-frills card with a 10 percent rate can save you $350 a year on a $5,000 balance.

Time Your Loans and Refinancing: One point on your interest rate could potentially save over a thousand dollars in interest on a loan. If you're getting a new mortgage or refinancing in an interest-rate environment where you think rates will fall, apply and then allow your rate to float for a while. Most lenders allow you to wait 30 days or more before locking in the interest rate you'll actually pay, so if you think rates are headed lower, take your time before locking – you may capture a lower rate. Conversely, if you think rates are heading up, lock immediately. Either way, get your rate in writing. A spoken agreement isn't worth much if your lender decides not to honor it.

Shop Around for a Mortgage: A good mortgage can save you thousands. When looking to buy a house or refinance your mortgage, take the time to apply for and compare several mortgage offers from a diverse set of sources: the institution where you do your day-to-day banking, a neighborhood bank, a credit union and an online lender. That way you can have confidence that you got the best terms possible. When comparing mortgage offers, don't forget to look at closing costs. Fees for things like title insurance and home inspections can vary greatly, even within the same institution. Taking time to compare or negotiate lower fees can save hundreds or even thousands of dollars, greatly reducing the real cost of your loan.

Nightlife & Social Spending

Date Creatively, Not Expensively: Dating can be a very expensive part of our lives. Dinner for two with drinks can easily top $150 if you want to go to a nice restaurant. Instead, think of something that will let you spend some quality time without breaking the bank. Browse a bookstore. Sketch portraits of each other. Take dance lessons. Have a picnic. Go to a lecture or performance at your local college. Do an internet search for free concerts or art exhibits.

Fill Up Before Going Out. I have a friend who is a young professional that recently made a big life change—he was living the high life with a high salary at an investment bank and then quit to work for a nonprofit. He is happier, but his budget was lacking, especially when it came to the several social outings a week he was accustomed to. He recently told me of a fix that he has: He buys a six-pack of bagels and a box of tea each week and skips the coffee shop. He also snacks on peanut butter and banana sandwiches before meeting up with friends at night so he can bypass the pricey entrees at restaurants, opting for cheaper appetizers instead. It saves him about $100 a week.

Party In Instead of Going Out: Game nights and movie nights at home have soared in popularity recently, which is no surprise given that a night out on the town means paying $8 or more for drinks and $50 or more when you include cab rides, cover charges, and meals. If you are creative, you can plan a night at your house or a friend's house that is as entertaining as it is inexpensive.

Automotive & Transportation

Avoid Unnecessary Teen Driver Charges: Make sure your teen studies hard – some auto insurers offer discounts to good students. If the child be driving a family car, designate which vehicle they will drive to avoid be charged as if they're driving the highest-risk vehicle on your policy. Lower the estimated monthly mileage on the vehicle they are insured on—they are probably only driving to school and social functions. And when they go off to college, take them off your insurance altogether to save big.
Buy and Sell Cars Efficiently: Consider buying a one- or two-year-old car. If the factory warranty is still good, you could get a car with 95 percent of its life left for 20 percent to 30 percent less than the cost of buying new. Be prepared to walk away from a deal. You know within a few hundred dollars what you should be paying, and every minute spent discussing a figure significantly higher than that is wasted. You should sell your old car privately, get someone else to assume the lease or stay with the thing until it's paid off. Don't roll negative equity into a new car loan.
Minimize Car Use: Look for ways to cut out your car altogether. Consider walking, biking or telecommuting. If you live in an area that has good public transportation, take advantage of it. Even if you can't quit driving altogether, using some of these methods, your family can get by on one car instead of two. You should also consider carpooling. Carpool matching services are available free in many communities. Do a search online for a local carpool center or call your local government.
Be Wise When Gassing Up: Don't top off the gas tank. Rapidly starting and stopping a gas pump can cause it to overcharge you for the small amount of gas you put in, and there's a good chance gas will slosh or seep out. Buy the lowest grade (octane) of gasoline that is appropriate for your car. As long as your engine doesn't knock or ping, the fuel you're using is fine. Research shows that increased MPG in higher octane gasoline is negligible and not cost-effective when you factor in the higher price.

Mothball One of Your Cars: Here is an interesting money-saving experiment for you.   If your household has two cars, try leaving one in the garage for a month. See how it affects your life. With a modest amount of planning, a lot of households might be able to make do with a single car. Once you've determined that you can do likewise, sell the second car, bank the money, and also begin enjoying lower bills for auto insurance, gasoline, and maintenance.

Maintain Your Car for Better Fuel Performance: Keeping tires inflated properly saves fuel and tread wear, and a well-tuned engine that gets regular oil changes burns less gas. Tighten the gas cap. And if your cap doesn't fit snugly, buy a new one. Gas easily evaporates from the tank if it has a way to escape. Lighten up on the accelerator, and don't make fast starts or sudden stops. The faster you drive the more gas you use. For example, driving at 55 mph rather than 65 mph can improve your fuel economy by two miles per gallon. The decreased wear on the engine will also pay dividends.

Grocery Expenses

This is an expense that every family faces, and most of the time it could be reduced drastically. As shown by a Bureau of Labor Statistics study, the average family spent $6443 on food. To shed a little more light on these statistics, we must take into account that the "average" family has 2.5 people and an income of $63,563. So the math is pretty simple-- the average family spends about 10% of their income on food.

Is that too much? You tell me. I'm not going to be so bold as to tell you how to feed your family, and eating habits can vary widely from household to household. I will, however, list some tips that I have heard from my clients and let you decide what will save your family money.

Know Where to Look: All grocery stores today place the most profitable items at eye level and on end of an aisle. Another place they will put high-grossing items is in the checkout lane. Sometimes finding a good deal is as simple as bending down—looking in places not directly in your line-of-sight.

Cook from Scratch: Making meals from scratch is probably the single best way to save on food. Because the more prepared the food, the more it costs. Ironically, less expensive home-made is also normally better for you as well. You would be amazed to see how little your sodium, cholesterol, and saturated fat intake is on a cooked-from-scratch meal compared to a prepared meal.

Cook in Larger Proportions: Make larger batches of food when you prepare a meal, and freeze what is not devoured that evening. The time you save by cooking a meal for two nights instead of one could be spent on making it from scratch, which will save money.

Making a List: Writing down what you came for…and ignoring everything not on it… will save money. Remember that grocery stores have made an art form out of marketing products that will give them the highest mark-up-- and get you to spend more of your hard-earned money. It will also save time and fuel expense by preventing repeat trips to the store for things you forgot.

Generics: sometimes generics aren't as good as name brands. In those situations one might choose name brands. But for things like flour, sugar, salt, bleach or virtually dozens of other items you find in the grocery store, the only discernible difference is price. Paying more for an identical product is more than extravagant; it's foolish.

Coupons: The thought of carefully scouring a Sunday newspaper and clipping coupons can make some nauseous. But many can attest to the incredible savings that coupons provide. These days' online coupons have made them easier to find and use. If you haven't used a coupon search engine yet, do so.

Avoiding Money Mistakes

The old adage "you have to spend money to make money" can be true in business, but when it comes to personal finances you may want to rethink the approach. Maybe instead you could think: You have to not spend money to save money. Of course, never spending any money at all isn't an option. I have, however, compiled a few of the most common mistakes that lead to the unnecessary spending of money.
The following items explain some of the common wastes of money that you could avoid or substitute without losing quality of life. Remember, the idea here is to maximize total utility of your money; not to live like a pauper to save a few shillings. Please review this section to see if there are any money mistakes that you could avoid.

Closing Your HELOC Early: Lenders have been quick to freeze or slash borrowers' home-equity lines of credit in the past few years. But if you dare close down a line yourself within the first three to four years of opening it, you'll pay from $250 to $700. Two-thirds of all lenders charge such fees, says Keith Gumbinger of HSH. He says it's because the creditor has to absorb certain closing costs. What you should do is leave the line open, even if you don't plan to use it. If you must close the line – say, because you want to refinance your mortgage – ask your lender to waive the fee. If the same lender has your HELOC and your new mortgage, it may comply. If you are persistent in speaking with them, these sorts of fees are always negotiable.
Paying Too Much in Annuity Fees: Expenses on these tax-deferred insurance products (the value of which depends on underlying investments you select) tend to run 2% to 3% annually. But it's nearly impossible to figure out exactly what you are paying. The fees are required to be disclosed in an annuity's prospectus, which can run hundreds of pages. Once you find the right page, you have to do some complicated math to figure total costs for the specific investments, riders, and features you choose. Because of the high fees, variable annuities rarely make sense. If you're interested in

retirement income, go with a lower cost immediate annuity. If its tax deferral you're seeking and you're already maxing out 401(k)s and IRAs, tax-efficient funds (such as index funds and ETFs) are a better bet. Already in a variable annuity? Check out the surrender charges – which can be as high as 10 percent—before switching.

Neglecting to Budget for the Long Term: It is easier to do short term budgeting because more of the variables are already understood. We know what cash we have on hand and know what our immediate needs are. Once we start budgeting long term, it gets more complicated because we must factor in unknowns (like a busted water heater or medical emergency). However, research suggests that creating an annual budget instead of a monthly one works best, largely because we feel less confident in our annual estimates, so we tend to add more cushioning for unexpected expenses. In one study, college students underestimated their monthly expenses by 40 percent while overestimating their annual expenses by 3 percent. This helps consumers to be more disciplined in their spending.

Failing to Make "Career Investments": Investing in a career coach or development course can help you snag a promotion, get "unstuck" from a career rut, or transition into your dream job. The price of one-on-one coaching typically starts at around $200 an hour (which I would not recommend unless you are confident in a return on your investment), but less formal advice can come from meeting with more experienced colleagues over lunch or coffee. Remember that a career investment does not necessarily mean spending cash, but you could put in some extra time to expand your skill set or meet with a mentor at work.

Too Much Debt... Or Too Little: Not all debt is bad. It can enable you to return to school, buy much-needed professional outfits before receiving your first paycheck, or even cover your rent during a tough month. Being so afraid of debt that you avoid it altogether can force you to miss out on opportunities, while taking on too much can lead to financial ruin. The key is to understand debt and use it responsibly. A basic rule of thumb is to never take on debt for something you won't get a return on. That is why a home mortgage isn't necessarily bad debt because we typically expect the property to appreciate. However, an auto loan could fall into this category if you need to have a vehicle to get to work and get income but don't have the cash on hand to buy one. Underestimating tax bills: People who earn money beyond their usual paycheck, from freelance work or a side business, are most at risk for owing a lot of money in April, which can also trigger additional fees. Married couples who earn similar, high salaries are also at risk, because of the so-called marriage penalty. Check to see if you've been paying roughly the correct amount of taxes by reviewing your payroll stubs or other documentation. If your taxes are simple and you only expect refunds in April rather than additional taxes, then the only worry you will have is making sure you exemptions are filled out accordingly so that the IRS doesn't hold too much of your money interest free. I will discuss this more in the Finance chapter of this book.

Paying to Get Credit Rewards Reinstated: Have a reward card? Some issuers have a creative new way of punishing you for paying late. They will take away the points you earned in that billing cycle – and make you fork over money to get them back. Diner's Club charges a $15 reinstatement fee; American Express, $29. Some other issuers, including Capital One, won't let you get your points back for any price. The easiest way to avoid this is to plan ahead so that late payments are not an issue. Schedule automatic payments online for at least the minimum amount due.

Reward Card Traps: Rewards credit cards sound good in theory, but in reality they encourage you to spend more than you would otherwise. Economists dub this phenomenon "purchase acceleration," because you ramp up your spending when that reward is in sight. Rewards cards also carry a higher interest rate—two percentage points, on average—than non-rewards cards. Reward cards can be a great way to make bonus cash or get free flights if your rewards are coming from money you would have spent anyway. But if you increase your spending habits for the sake of the reward, you are falling victim to their marketing.

You Need to Haggle: Even department stores often offer some wiggle room on their posted prices, and big-box stores usually match competitors' prices. This negotiating trend has become so prevalent that there is actually a modern name coined for it: neo-haggling. But many consumers fail to realize that prices are flexible and don't bother asking for a better deal. If you are persistent, you will be surprised to see how much this can save you.

Closing Fees for Your Brokerage Account: No matter how unhappy you may be with your broker, you seem even more unhappy to discover that you'll have to shell out to sever your relationship. Many of the major firms – such as Fidelity, Schwab, and WellsTrade – charge transfer fees, generally between $50 and $200, if you close your account and move your money to a different firm. If your current brokerage is holding you hostage with its fee, appeal to the company where you want to move your funds. Many will reimburse you. To prevent these problems down the road, when you first sign up at a brokerage, ask that it waive such fees. These things are negotiable, especially if you have a sizable account.

Overspending on housing: It's almost impossible to get ahead financially unless you save a significant chunk of your income—ideally, $1 of every $3 you earn. But many people get tripped up by their housing costs. Traditionally, financial advisors have encouraged buyers to spend about one-third of their income on housing. But for many people, especially anyone with student loan debts, child care payments, or other hefty expenses, that's too much money. So instead of following the "One-Third Rule" blindly, make a long-term budget and factor in the savings you want before accounting for housing. Then you will see what you can *really* afford for housing-- it may be less than one-third.

Charged for Not Charging: A few credit card issuers have started levying annual fees on less active users to encourage them to spend. Citibank, for example, slaps a $60 fee on certain cardholders unless they charge $2,400 within a year. And US Bank Visa Platinum dings you $40 if you don't use your card during a 12-month period. Happily, such fees are the exception, not the rule. So vote with your wallet—look into switching to a card issued by a credit union. Credit unions typically charge fewer fees than big banks do.

Neglecting Other Sources of Income: The average worker now holds 10 different jobs before age 36. While some of those job changes are voluntary, many also come from layoffs. By earning income from a variety of sources, workers can increase their financial stability. Options for new sources of income include freelance work, a teaching gig at a local community college, or a potentially money-making blog. Many resources are out there to help you set up a website if you feel you have a product or service that others would be willing to pay for. Selling on eBay has also become a hobby of many that are looking to earn a little extra on the side.

Getting Things for Free

When you are trying to save money, there is nothing better than finding something you need for my favorite price—free. This section is a compilation of goods and services that are possible to find for free if you know where to look. I hope you find something that will save you money.

Basic Tax Preparation: If your tax situation isn't that complicated, then you should probably be preparing your own tax return using one of the many free online services. It's now common for e-filing to be free as well with many services. You won't even need a stamp. Each year just look around in the IRS.gov site where you file your 1040 EZ form.
Budgeting Tools: There are many budgeting tools (both online and desktop) that offer up the service for free. Don't ask me how they do this, but who cares. If you're looking to reign in some of your spending, the good news is you can do it for free. This is a great place to start if you feel overwhelmed with trying to get a budget going.
Basic Computer Software: Thinking of purchasing a new computer? Think twice before you fork over the funds for a bunch of extra software. There are some great alternatives to the name

brand software programs. The most notable is OpenOffice, the open-source alternative to those other guys. It's completely free and files can be exported in compatible formats.

Free Business Advice: Run your own business and you're bound to have questions. Go to SCORE.org to get free, confidential small-business advice. The nonprofit has 12,400 volunteer counselors, who are working and retired executives and business owners. Drop in to one of SCORE's 364 offices nationwide for a face-to-face consultation, or chat with an expert online. Another great resource is the Small Business Administration. It often hosts free local workshops, and its Web site (SBA.gov) has an extensive list of tools and resources for entrepreneurs.

Free Checking: At many banks, free checking is soon to become fee checking. But plenty of banks still offer free checking accounts. SunTrust, for example, offers a free plan with no minimum balance required. And you get free online and ATM service too. Wachovia and U.S. Bank still have their own version of free accounts. Chase even offers $100 for opening such an account. Indeed, a host of banks and savings and loans offer free checking. So far. When you're looking for lower fees, including free checking, always to look to smaller local banks and credit unions.

Free Bill Pay: If you're still shelling out for a bill-paying service, it's time to quit. (At $10 per month, you're throwing away $120 per year.) Same goes for those of you still paying for stamps and snail-mailing your payments. (If you mail five bills per month, you're spending more than $26 per year on postage, simply for the privilege of paying your bills!) Many banks offer free bill paying with their online checking accounts. Even if yours doesn't, you can usually pay everything from phone bills to property taxes by electronic check through the biller's Web site at no extra charge. You may even sign up for free automatic payments or e-mail reminders to ensure you never get slapped with a late fee.

Free Education: Many colleges and universities, such as Johns Hopkins, University of Notre Dame and Massachusetts Institute of Technology, post course material and lectures on their Web sites. You won't get credit toward a degree, but you can pursue an interest, sharpen your skills or even learn a language. You can also go to Apple's iTunes U to access more than 250,000 free lectures, videos and other materials from 600 universities, including Oxford, Stanford and Yale.

Cell Phone: The service plan may be expensive, but the phone itself doesn't have to cost a thing. Most major carriers will give you a free phone, even a free smart phone, with a two-year contract.

Books: There's a cool place in your town that's renting out books for free: the library. Remember that place? Stop by and put your favorite book on reserve. And if you don't feel like getting out, visit paperbackswap.com and find your books there (small shipping fees apply).

Free Credit Reports: You can go to AnnualCreditReport.com for a free look at your credit history once a year. If the Financial Regulatory Reform bill passes, you might also one day get a look at your credit score. Read about other changes ahead here.

The News: Traditional print is a waste of paper and delivery resources. I'm not anti-newspaper. I just don't find them practical anymore. Skip the daily 50 cents and get your news online. And for you dedicated coupon clippers, you can get most of your Sunday coupons online now too.

Free Cash: If you can't find an ATM near you for a free cash withdrawal, no worries: Plenty of stores will give you cash back with no fee when you use your ATM card to make even a small purchase. You can buy a candy bar or a Diet Coke and get back up to $100 in cash from Wal-Mart. Target will give you back $40 if you use your ATM card for a purchase. Grocery stores also offer cash back. And then there are iPhone and other apps that will help you locate ATMs.

Free Phone Assistant: Streamline your personal phone system with Google Voice, a free service that allows people to dial one phone number to ring all your phones simultaneously. It converts voice-mail messages to text that you can go back to and search by keyword (no more Post-It collages on the wall). You can set up different voice-mail greetings for different callers, plus you can easily screen or block calls – all without paying for a personal assistant.

Exercise: Skip the expensive gym memberships. Visit your local park for a walk or run. Do basic push-up and sit-up programs in your living room. Rent a workout DVD from the library. There are many free workout programs you can download online as well.
Free Tech Support: If you're a member of Sam's Club or Costco, you can get free tech support – even if you didn't buy the device at their store. Or, for PC problems, anyone can head to TechGuy.org or 5starsupport.com for free help. You can search the forums for your computer's particular ailment or post a question to receive a timely response from the sites' groups of geek volunteers. And don't forget to try the manufacturer's website. Many post user manuals and FAQs to help you solve your dilemma.
Free Information Call: Google 411 will get you information numbers free, so don't get ripped off by your cell phone provider. When you need directory assistance, dial 800-GOOG-411.
Free Scholarship Search: Plenty of websites offer free searches for scholarships, such as Fastweb. There's even a company called Free Scholarship Searches that offers links to 40 websites that offer free scholarship searches.
Free e-Books: If you own a Kindle, iPad or other electronic reader, you can populate your e-library without breaking the bank. E-books commonly sell for $9.99 – less than hard covers but about as much as paperbacks. But at Gutenberg.org, you won't pay a cent to download about 33,000 classics whose copyrights have expired, including War and Peace, Moby Dick and Little Women.
Music: You can download music for free off the Internet—and you can also get in a lot of trouble for it. As for some legal strategies to getting your tunes gratis, streaming radio stations like Pandora, Grooveshark and Jango let you tailor stations to suit your taste, while MySpace has an impressive collection of full-length albums you can listen to for free.
Travel Lodging: This is not for the faint of heart. People around the world are willing to let you stay in their homes for free. CouchSurfing.org connects weary travelers with open couches. Just decide where you want to go, find some hosts, read their profiles and reviews from people who've stayed with them

before, and get in touch. The site forbids any formal commercial transactions, but cooking dinner for your host or cleaning the living room is generally polite and appreciated.

Free Baggage: Sure, nearly all airlines are charging to check baggage but at least one doesn't: Southwest. And remember carrying on bags is still free, except for on Spirit Airlines.

Free Entertainment: Your local library and parks offer lots of free fun, from books to movies to concerts. Join their e-mail list to see what's up. And of course, there's the Internet, offering free games as well as magazine and newspaper articles. Just go to the website of your favorite periodical.

Free Water: While technically not free, tap water is about as close as you can get. If you're concerned about water quality, buy a filter. But don't ever pay for water at a convenience store.

Free Car-Repair Help: It won't fix your car free, but RepairPal.com will help you find out whether your mechanic is quoting a fair price. Enter your car's make, model and year, plus your zip code. Then choose among dozens of fixes to get a price range for the job at dealerships and independent shops in your area.

Antibiotics: There is still no cure for the common cold, but for bacterial afflictions, like ear infections, strep throat and severe acne, there are some economically painless remedies. Many pharmacies around the country, including Stop & Shop, Publix and ShopRite, offer free generic antibiotics to anyone with a prescription. Giving away relatively cheap, short-term medicines in hopes of hooking customers on higher-margin items is a common practice.

Credit Card: With as many credit cards as there are available on the market today, it's easy to avoid a credit card with an annual fee. Unless you're dead set on a particular perk that a fee card brings, skip the annual fee card and pocket that money yourself.

Debt Reduction Help: Speaking of credit cards, if you're in over your head with credit card help, there are many free sources you can turn to for help with your debt. No one is going to be able to magically wipe away your debts, but there is help out there that will set you up on a debt reduction plan you can handle. Start with a visit to the National Foundation for Credit Counseling.

Free TV: Thanks to sites like Hulu, you can now watch many popular television shows online for free. If your favorite shows are free on the web, why pay for cable or satellite? Doing a video search for your favorite TV show will typically lead you where you need to be to watch any show you would like.

Free Passport Photos: You'll pay about $15 at the post office to get your picture taken for your passport. Instead, take your photo with your own digital camera then upload it to ePassportPhoto.com, which will help you size it properly before printing it on your home printer. The best part: You can redo your picture as many times as you like to get it right. After all, who wants to get stuck with a bad photo for the next 10 years?

Pets: This is a controversial one, I know. But there are likely many pets down at your local animal shelter that could use just as much love as the pure-bred types. There may be a small fee due to the shelter for shots and basic care, but you'll have your pet home without paying a mini-fortune. Besides, theoretically it is better to save an animal at a shelter than buying one from a pet store or dealer in a system that often will breed animals in less-than-humane conditions.

Video Editing Software: Windows Live Movie Maker and Google Picasa are good free choices for basic video editing. (Apple's iMovie software that comes on your Mac will also do the job.) They each let you assemble clips; add transitions, titles, music and more with ease. You can then post your video to social networking sites, download it to your computer or burn it onto a DVD. You might also consider Pixorial.com. This simple online-based editor lets you invite friends and family to collaborate on your project, and allows you to save up to 10GB of video free of charge.

Free Telephone Calls: Services like Skype and AIM let you communicate with other users for free. Always calling a loved one long distance? If you both get copies of something like Skype, you can talk all you want without paying a dime. And with a service like Google Voice, you can get all of your cell phone calls free, too.

Free Wi-Fi: About 6,800 Starbucks and 11,500 McDonald's nationwide recently began offering free Wi-Fi. Other restaurants like Panara Bread and Atlanta Bread have made Wi-Fi standard as well. You can also go to WiFiFreeSpot.com to find places to surf free when you're away from home. The database includes airports, restaurants, hotels and more.

Real Estate

When it comes to saving money, your home is one of the largest considerations that you will have to take. Over the course of your life, the expenses of your living quarters are going to take a huge portion of all the money you ever spend, thus, if you spend that money wisely there is potential for huge savings.

Economic Outlook

Before you make any decisions regarding your real estate spending, it is important to gauge what has happened recently and what the real estate market has in store for us. Nobody knows exactly where the real estate market will be in 5 years, but some background information and general understanding on the effects of the real estate market can save you thousands of dollars if you avoid a major error in real estate spending.

The main drive of the most recent economic boom was due to the real estate bubble. Property values were at the highest they had ever been, making property owners all much wealthier on paper. This inspired consumer confidence and everyone was spending their money and lots of it—a surefire cause for economic boom. But the real estate collapse took those gains away and then some and halted the boom and drove it down to lows we hadn't seen since the dotcom bust of 2001-2002. The economy is beginning to pick up and regain its losses, but the real estate market is expected to hold it back rather than push it forward.

Despite clear signs of an upturn in the larger economy, including a revival in manufacturing and consumer spending, the nation's market for homes and office buildings remains sluggish because of foreclosures and oversupply. That disproportion will be worked out over time, but in the meantime, it is slowing the recovery in many ways.

Construction jobs have struggled because of the lack of new projects. Construction is a big employer and one of the higher-paid sectors for men who lack a college degree. The sector has shed 2.1 million jobs from its peak in March 2007 to April 2010. The 5.6 million construction jobs that are left comprise 4% of U.S. jobs, down from 6% when employment peaked in December 2007.

With the oversupply of houses, offices and malls already pressuring the real-estate market, many of these jobs will not come back for a while, putting added pressure on unemployment even as growth continues.

Home owners who once felt rich are feeling poorer. Throughout the boom, consumers used their home equity to borrow and spend as they watched housing prices escalate. The ratio of dollars taken out of homes to total personal income—a gauge of how much consumers are pulling out of their homes relative to how much they make in wages and other income—fell the last three quarters of 2009. During the boom years, that ratio got as high as 9% nationwide.

While real-estate prices have stabilized, they are unlikely to regain pre-recession values for years. That has left many consumers with a pile of debt but not much home equity to be used for investment or spending, a big reason why economists believe recent gains in consumer spending aren't sustainable.

Small businesses aren't borrowing as much. While bigger companies can access the now-recovered market for bonds and other debt, many smaller companies—which are key job generators—use the value of their own property to secure bank loans. As the value of those holdings has fallen, so too has their ability to get loans, crimping investment and hiring at a time when the recovery is gaining steam.

About half of small businesses own at least part of the commercial buildings in which they are located, and the majority of them have mortgages, according to the National Federation of Independent Business. But as real-estate values have fallen, so has this source of equity, limiting how much a bank can lend them.

U.S. nonfinancial companies had $6.3 trillion in real-estate assets at the end of 2009, down 33% from 2007, according to the Federal Reserve. That drop is a big reason why corporations' total net worth fell to $12.9 trillion from $15.9 trillion over the same period-- a 19 percent decrease.

With the value of property (which is often used as collateral for loans) so depressed "the ability for many small employers to borrow will be constrained precisely as sales begin to strengthen and new investments are warranted," wrote the National Federation of Independent Business in a report on small-business credit conditions.

Lower real-estate values translate into lower property taxes, crimping government spending. State and local governments employ 20 million police officers, teachers and other employees, roughly 15% of the work force and more than in all of manufacturing. But much of the money to provide services and pay employees comes from property taxes, which depend on property values. Even as the economy and job market recover, Local governments are cutting employees as they grapple with the worst budget deficits in a generation.

Property taxes continued to grow through the recession and recovery, in part because local governments calculate the levy based on property assessments that are often years old. Property taxes grew 5.7% to $170 billion in the last three months of 2009 versus the same period in 2008. That won't last as tax assessments catch up with reality.

In California, one of the first states into recession, Santa Barbara County saw its 2009 property taxes decline for the first time since 1978. This means that property tax income has only just begun to slump. Imagine the effect that this will have on municipalities that are already strapped for cash.

Now we can see the vast effects that real estate has had on the rest of the economy. Let's talk more about what we like most—saving money.

Buying a Foreclosed Home

We've all seen it in the news: All over the country homes are being foreclosed on by lenders. This happens when I person buys a home with a loan from a lending institution but fails to make their payments and the lending institution takes the property back. With the real estate crash and following economic recession, homes have been foreclosed on at a rate we have never before seen.

To rid themselves of growing inventory of properties, Fannie Mae and Freddie Mac (huge, quasi-government mortgage lending institutions) are scrambling to unload hundreds of thousands of foreclosed homes. And that means incredible deals-- like requiring as little as 3% down, offering to pay a portion of the closing costs and arranging special financing and warranties for repairs and renovations.

It's another option for home owners who want to trade up — and an easier way into the market for first-time home buyers. The best bargain might be the home's price, and that is the best place to start. A friend of mine and savvy real estate investor always tells me, "In real estate, you make your money on the buy, not the sell." What he means is this: If you buy a property at a good price, you're setting yourself up for almost certain profit in the future.

The downside: Angry neighbors. These types of listings are devaluing nearby properties. That means in some areas where Freddie and Fannie homes are on the market, buyers could find a better deal on a nearby market-rate home that doesn't require repairs.

Buying a Fannie or Freddie home can be more complex than pursuing an open-market real estate listing — or even a commercial bank foreclosed property. There's a smaller selection of appealing properties, or properties that don't require renovation work.

The three best features of Fannie and Freddie foreclosures that make digging for these deals worthwhile:
Small Down Payment: For its foreclosed properties, Fannie Mae will accept down payments as low as 3% on 30-year mortgages at the same interest rates banks are currently offering. And Fannie Mae doesn't require private mortgage insurance. Compared to a typical bank mortgage, which requires 10% down, plus PMI for buyers with less than 20%, that's a huge savings — an estimated $51,000 up front and upwards of $2,500 per year PMI on a $300,000 mortgage.
It's a tradeoff, though. For buyers with 20% down, mortgage payments on a 30-year mortgage loan at 5% would be $1,288 a month. With just 3% down, the buyer would need to borrow $291,000 and make a $1,562 monthly payment.
Help with Renovations: Fannie and Freddie have fixed big flaws like leaky roofs and damaged electrical work, and they often handle small projects like replacing appliances that are broken or missing, tearing up old carpet, or fixing other damage left by former owners or vandals.
Now, to entice buyers who want to update or upgrade, many of Fannie Mae's properties come with an optional mortgage that includes extra financing up to $30,000 for repairs and improvements. But with a little down payment and the extra amount tacked on, the buyer could end up owing more than the house is worth — especially if home prices continue to drop.
Priority for Home-buyers Rather than Investors: Buyers who plan to live in their Freddie Mac-purchased home will get to see properties for at least the first 15 days they're on the market — before the listing opens to would-be landlords. Many bank-owned foreclosure properties are snatched up by cash-stocked investors who can wait out the downturn to sell later at a profit.
And Fannie and Freddie homes can be seen inside and out — unlike some regular foreclosure listings. Consider bringing along a contractor when you view the home to help spot areas that need repairs and provide pricing. (Most contractors will do this for free.)

Protecting Your Investment

For most people, a home is one of the most valuable assets they'll ever own. Unfortunately, there are some major perils that can befall a house and put a serious dent in the value of that asset. Please consider the following issues when you are planning on purchasing a home or evaluating your existing home.
Foundation: If you have bowed basement walls, cracks in walls or floors or a tilting chimney, you may be aware that these are signs of a problem foundation. But many people don't realize that difficulty opening and closing doors and windows can also be early signs that your home is shifting. And whether you have a new home or an old one, foundation problems often require major repairs -- and a big cash outlay. Foundation problems can be caused by the type of soil the house is built on, an improperly laid foundation or drainage problems. Whatever the cause, a bad foundation is bad news and, depending on the severity of the problem, can cost the homeowner well over $10,000.
Solutions: Assuming your home was properly built, the most you can do to prevent problems in your foundation is to ensure that your home has proper drainage. This means that gutters and eaves troughs should be kept clear and in good repair, and your yard should be properly graded to ensure that water runs away from your house.
Mold: Unlike major water damage, such as that caused by flooding, minor or hidden water damage in your home, perhaps from a defective water pipe, hot water heater or window seal, can cause just as much damage -- and you may not notice it right away. Similarly, if your home suffered through a flood in the past and did not adequately dry out, mold can also thrive. (If you live in a flood-prone area, flood insurance is a must.)
A 2005 study by the National Resources Defense Council showed that New Orleans homes that had been flooded or were even near areas of flooding showed extremely high levels of mold spores that could pose health threats to residents, even in the homes that had been repaired and treated for mold. And the more humid the area in which you live, the harder it will be for

you to get rid of mold and keep it from coming back. According to the Environmental Protection Agency, if the mold growth in your home is larger than 10 square feet or was caused by sewage or other contaminated water; it's time to call in a professional. Although home insurance may cover some of the costs depending on your policy, the cost of mold remediation is about $3,000 per wall, according to Environmental Solutions Group, an environmental management company that inspects homes for mold -- and that doesn't include the cost of replacing any mold-infected materials such as drywall, carpet or ceiling tiles.
Solutions: Mold can't grow without moisture, so it's important that you check for and fix any leaks in your home immediately, use fans in kitchens and bathrooms to vent moisture outside and clean up any mold growth immediately to prevent it from spreading.
Water Damage: If your home isn't water tight, this isn't something you can ignore. Beyond the possibility of mold, long-term water damage can cause rot, which can lead to all kinds of expensive repairs to the structure of your home. It's difficult to estimate the cost of this type of repair, but it can easily run into the thousands depending on how much wood needs to be replaced and how intrusive the repairs are.
Solutions: Be vigilant about water damage in your home; if you find leaks or areas that tend to be damp, have them repaired before long-term damage occurs. If you find rotten wood in your home, repair the problem before it gets out of hand.
Bedbugs: If you're a homeowner rather than a renter, you may think you're immune to this one. Not so. A recent nationwide infestation of bedbugs has seen the little blood-sucking critters popping up all over the place -- including movie theaters, office buildings and hotels, making it very easy for anyone to bring the infestation home. And, because many of the most effective chemicals for killing bedbugs have been found to be dangerous, eliminating the spread is harder than ever.
Solutions: Avoid bringing home used furniture, mattresses or bedding. If you travel, inspect your hotel carefully for bed bugs (even upscale hotels have suffered from this problem), and avoid

placing your luggage on the floor. If you find bed bugs in your home, contact an exterminator.

Sewer Line Problems: The portion of the sewer line that extends out from a home and onto city property is often the homeowners' responsibility when it comes to repairs. Sewer line problems are most common in older neighborhoods, where the line may have sagged or has been damaged by tree roots. If you have slow running or gurgling drains, frequent backups in your plumbing system or sewage smells outside your home, these may be indications of a problem. Again, your home insurance policy may cover this cost, expect this doozy to cost anywhere from $5,000 to $15,000 for a 100-foot sewer pipe.

Solutions: If you experience signs of sewer problems in your home, have a professional inspect your lines. Clogs and tree roots can often be removed at a lower cost, without complete replacement of the pipe.

Renting vs. Buying

People will tell you that if you are renting a property rather than owning, you are throwing money away each month when you could be building equity in a property you own and are paying a mortgage on instead. This is true in many circumstances. If you purchase a property in an area where you plan to stay for several years, you expect the value of the property to appreciate steadily, and you expect your income to be stable and sufficient to pay the mortgage each month- then it is a good idea to purchase. You must also consider your ability to negotiate a good rate on a home loan (a solid credit score with lengthy credit history will do the trick) and whether a property you have targeted is actually in your means.

There are, however, circumstances where renting is a better idea. Naturally, renting is a better option if you will be living in an area temporarily, property values are falling rather than rising, or your income is unstable. There are also circumstances where the values of properties are too inflated in relation to rental rates in the area. Today this can be the case in parts of Southern California, San Francisco, Phoenix, Las Vegas and large parts of Florida, the Pacific Northwest and the Northeast.

An adult that is financially secure and established will often be second guessed by their friends and real estate agents alike. As you know, it may not always be a question of dollars and cents, but the pride of owning property. In my opinion, there is little pride in missing the opportunity to save thousands of dollars a year if your situation fits the right equation.

In some markets that were recently a bubble, prices have fallen so far that buying a home appears to be a bargain, based on a recent analysis of prices and rents in 48 metropolitan areas. In South Florida, Phoenix and Las Vegas, house prices — relative to rents — are as low as in places that had not been outrageously inflated, like Indianapolis and St. Louis.

But in a handful of other areas, including Portland, Seattle and San Francisco, house prices remain significantly higher than they were before the real estate bubble started. People who buy a home in these areas will face higher monthly costs than if they rented, even when all of the tax benefits are considered. If you buy a home in such an area, you are in effect betting that the value of your home is going to appreciate quickly and steadily enough to offset the savings you would make by renting instead.

The country's two biggest metropolitan areas, New York and Los Angeles, are a perfect example of today's schizophrenic real estate market. Average house prices across both areas have fallen enough that buying may now be a good deal for many consumers. Yet there are still significant pockets where renting looks like a more prudent option — including parts of Manhattan, the New York suburbs and Orange County, Calif.

Eric G., a physician's assistant in Las Vegas, plans to close on his first home purchase — a four-bedroom, $170,000 house nearly identical to the one he is now renting — in the next few days. He decided to buy, he said, when he found out he could save money by doing so. "I didn't buy a house when everyone did," said Eric, who lives with his girlfriend and their children. "So I suppose I am taking advantage of a market depressed by all of the foreclosures."

The analysis of these real estate markets is based on comparing the costs of buying and renting a similar home, using data from Moody's Economy.com, a research firm, and from real estate agents. This kind of comparison can never tell someone for sure what the best financial move will be. But it does show whether a buyer will need a big jump in future prices to cover all the costs of owning — including the down payment, closing costs, property taxes, mortgage interest, repairs and co-op fees.

A simple way to do the comparison is to look at something called the rent ratio: the purchase price of a house divided by the annual cost of renting a similar one. The number 20 provides a useful rule of thumb. When you do the math, you discover that a ratio above 20 means you should at least consider renting, especially if you may move again in the next five years or so. When the ratio is well below 20, the case for buying becomes a lot stronger.

In many large metropolitan areas, including New York, Los Angeles, Chicago, Houston, Dallas, Atlanta and South Florida, the average ratio is now 16 or lower. It was more than 25 in several of these places at the peak of the bubble, in 2006. With a ratio as low as 16 and interest rates as low as they are, the costs of owning can be less than the costs of renting — and the only way that buying a home hurts you financially is if the value of the property continues to drop.

A three-bedroom Victorian townhouse in San Francisco, Calif., for example, recently went on the market for $1.1 million, according to an online search. Including taxes, condo fees and the tax deduction for mortgage interest, a typical buyer making a 20 percent down payment would face an effective monthly payment of about $6,000. Compare that with the monthly rent on a similar three-bedroom condo nearby — $7,800. The math here would encourage me to buy, even in a market like San Francisco.

The equation works out similarly in less costly areas, too, even if they were previously booming cities like Phoenix and Orlando, Fla.; Midwestern cities like Minneapolis and Cleveland; or the outer-ring suburbs of most big cities. Much of New York

City's suburban areas seem to fall into this category as well.

The problem for potential buyers is that many real estate agents argue for buying even in places where the numbers don't add up. According to recent listings, the ratio in many areas falls around 28-32-- an obvious "don't buy" situation. Real estate agents make more money selling you a home than placing you in a rental, so obviously they are incentivized to encourage you to buy even if it may be financially unsound to do so.

The rent ratio has long been higher in New York and Los Angeles than most places, perhaps because of zoning rules or because the cities are home to large numbers of affluent households willing to pay extra to own. So it's possible that prices will not fall. But they are already high enough that the monthly costs of owning often exceed the cost of renting — even without taking into account the down payment or all of the closing costs, taxes, and liability you are taking on as a home owner.

A big reason is that prices still haven't fallen much in some places. In Huntington Beach Ca., the average per-square-foot sale price was only 9 percent lower early this year than at its 2007 peak. Some similarly affluent parts of the New York, Miami and San Diego areas have experienced declines of 25 to 50 percent.

Obviously, owning a home brings benefits that are not strictly financial. There is pride in owning property. Building equity in a home is a great way to gain net worth and solid credit-worthiness. It offers stability and, for many people, comfort. In 2008, when property values were falling and the bottom was not yet in sight, I still advised many of my clients to purchase a home (mostly because the ratios where they lived had fallen as low as 14). Even in Manhattan, San Francisco or Seattle, a family confident that it will stay put for a decade or more may well be wise to buy today.

But it's worth remembering that the advantages of homeownership are frequently exaggerated. The mortgage-interest tax deduction doesn't eliminate the cost of borrowing money; it merely reduces it. The freedom to paint your house any color you wish comes with the responsibility of paying for a new roof when the time comes. The savings you plan to make by owning a property over as long as 20 years can instantly be wiped out when you consider the fact that the real estate agent's fees alone could be in the tens of thousands.

I am always baffled when clients of mine don't even take renting as an option, even with the recent history of home values that were nearly cut in half in the course of less than a year. Do yourself a favor and accurately compare the costs of renting and buying when moving to a new area. The numbers never lie.

Not of the Faint of Heart: Living Rent-Free

Housing costs eat up a huge portion of anyone's budget. If you are interested in experimenting with some alternative living arrangements to bring those costs down to nothing, here are some options that you might consider.

House-sitting: I have friends that are currently living in Pasadena, Ca. in a spacious five-bedroom house with an ample backyard and stylish furnishings on a quiet tree-lined street. Amazingly, the house is not their own, but they are living in it completely free of rent-- they are house- sitting for a UCLA professor away on sabbatical. This is their fifth house-sitting gig since they moved to the area eight months ago. Rentals in the area for smaller, unfurnished homes range from $2,250 to $3,000 a month, so if they keep it up they will have saved over $30,000 by the time this book is published.

Whether homeowners have multiple properties, or they're taking an extended vacation or sabbatical, they may be looking for someone to watch and maintain their home while they're away and offer a free or drastically discounted place to stay in exchange. You can search for house sitting opportunities at HouseCarers.com (you'll pay $35 for 12 months of access to listings), SabbaticalHomes.com (free to view listings) and Caretaker Gazette ($30 for 12 months). Some of the gigs may ask you take on yard care and pet sitting responsibilities, or pay a small token of rent, but you can search for opportunities that match your skills and comfort level. You can place ads at the above sites as well as on your local Craigslist site and in community newspapers.

House sitting isn't entirely free, though. My friends pay $200 a month to rent a storage facility for their belongings, $50 to $100 a month to advertise their services, $100 a month for a cell phone they wouldn't otherwise use and $28 per semester for a post-office mail box. But that leaves plenty left over to chalk up to savings. If you find a good fit, the savings available are worth living in someone else's house and basically watering plants, taking out the trash and making sure the home doesn't look vacant.

Apartment Managing: You also might consider apartment management. In exchange for maintaining an apartment building and handling residents, you could get discounted or free rent. This could be a lot of responsibility, so make sure you are up to the task before signing up. You can usually find apartment management opportunities among job listings.

Home Sharing: Several cities nationwide offer non-profit home-sharing programs that match tenants with elderly homeowners who have a spare room but need a little extra cash, say, to cover rising property taxes or to help pay the mortgage after a spouse dies. Such programs are usually coordinated through local senior centers or the National Shared Housing Resource Center.

These match-up programs thoroughly screen tenants and some arrangements may require you to provide services in exchange for a rent reduction -- cooking, cleaning or providing transportation, for example.

Roommate bartering: A similar but longer-term arrangement is the role of live-in housekeeper. Increasingly, single working adults and empty nesters are taking on rent-free roommates in exchange for their services cooking meals, cleaning the house and maintaining the yard. You can arrange such "barter roommate" or "room maid" positions through popular roommate sites such as RoommateExpress.com and Craigslist.

Not surprisingly, however, some roommate bartering arrangers may have ulterior motives -- for example, a man looking for a female room maid may actually be looking for a relationship. And you could also find yourself in a situation where your landlord is requiring more work of you than you expected. It's important to protect yourself in both situations. Before entering a barter agreement, both parties should run background checks on the other. Put your arrangement in writing, including the duties and services you will provide. This will come in handy in case you end up in small claims court over a dispute. Remember to specify amounts and keep track of how much work you put in for rent. If you go over the agreed-upon amount, renegotiate with your landlord.

Moving in with Parents: With the economic recession and unemployment the highest since the Great Depression, it is not surprising to see this as a growing trend. Many twenty-somethings that have graduated school but have not yet landed their dream-job have been able to start saving money by moving back in with mom and dad. This, of course, does not come without drawbacks, but it is always something to consider.

Boosting Your Existing Home Value

If you are planning to purchase a home but plan to sell an existing home in the process, one of your best bets of coming out on top in this transaction is getting more money out of your existing home. Getting less than an optimal price out of your house is in effect wasting money that could be made. Be wary while doing this, as many popular pre-sale renovations can be a money-pit. Look for the changes that will give you the most return on what you pay. There are lots of relatively simple and affordable things you can do to give your home a facelift. Your house will look better and you will feel better about not sinking $25,000 into finishing a basement that may or may not add $25,000 to your sell.

Painting, especially if you are able to do it yourself, can be an inexpensive way of updating. A fresh coat of light pain on the interior walls can work wonders. Paint will always clean up dirty walls and give a room a better image. Although dark colors can be stylish, most experts advise a home seller to use lighter shades to brighten things up. Smart color selections can make a small or cramped room appear dramatically larger. In the foyer, make a good first impression with similar tones mixed at different strengths. In the living room, a bold color paired with a white ceiling makes the room seem taller than it really is.

     Good, well-maintained flooring can set a positive tone for the entire interior of your home. Take proactive steps to protect your biggest investment. Like paint, flooring can help create an impression of spaciousness and airiness. Whether it's a floating laminate floor, tile or a natural "green" alternative, lighter-tone flooring can make formerly drab areas appear modern and streamlined.

     Old windows aren't just ugly - they can also let your heat and air conditioning escape, costing you big bucks. While window treatments are typically a focus in many home makeovers, the actual windows themselves are often overlooked. However, upgrading old single-pane windows with new ENERGY STAR-qualified windows can save an average of between $126 and $465 per year on energy bills, and some new windows qualify for a federal tax credit.

     Neglected bushes and overgrown lawns can kill a home's curb appeal. Don't worry - you don't need a green thumb to spruce up your yard. Going green doesn't have to damage your finances. Clean up the site by removing any dead or dying plants, branches and flowers. Prune overgrown shrubs along the home's foundation so they are below the window sills and off walkways and driveways. Fill empty holes with site-appropriate plants. Have all the planting beds weeded, edged and mulched for a clean, crisp look. Finally, weed and fertilize the lawn and provide supplemental watering if necessary to maintain a lush green carpet of grass.

     While you're outside, there are a few other quick moves that can make a big difference. If you only have $1,000 to spend, what can you do that will get you the most return on your investment? One of your options could be adding color with paint to outdoor features such as window frames, decorative beams and porches. Stick with calm colors that complement the home's exterior color scheme, avoiding shocking shades and drastic contrasts. Clean external brickwork or concrete slabs with a liquid masonry cleaner to make them look new and neat. Power washing can give external stonework, walkways and front stoops a quick makeover and renting a power washer can often be quite cheap (less than $20 a day last time I rented).

Finally, you should scope out the front door. It's one of the first things people will notice in a home, so make it count. But that doesn't mean you have to break the bank because there are good options at every price level. You can paint it for the cost of your time and a little paint or have it professionally replaced for $1,000 or more.

Which is more expensive: Urban or Suburban living?

When a person is moving, especially when the move is related to a job in a metro area, the question often comes up: Would it be better to live in the city or in the suburbs? Or maybe you've been living in the city for years, but you just had your second child and the apartment is getting a little cramped. Should you go spread out on a suburban parcel?

But that would mean leaving friends behind, along with easy access to work, the theater, great ethnic restaurants and just the general stimulation of urban living. The prospect of more space, however, is tempting — a bedroom for each child, a lawn to stretch out on. And there's the luxury of simply pulling into a driveway and a reputable public school just around the corner.

Which to choose?

In the end, deciding which lifestyle best suits you — and where to buy — comes down to personal preferences. But if the deciding factor is the relative cost of each, the answer is quantifiable, even if it not immediately obvious given the different tax rates and other variables.

I did the math for myself when I was thinking of heading

for wider pastures, and then recently looked into it for a friend of mine. Although the two samples were 12 years apart, the results were staggeringly similar-- both claiming suburban living to be more expensive by 17% and 18% respectively. Even a house in the suburbs with a price tag substantially lower than an urban apartment will, on a monthly basis, often cost more to keep running. And then there's the higher cost of commuting from the suburbs, or the expense of buying a car (or two) and paying the insurance.

There is a bit of a curve-ball in the equation. Many parents that are living downtown would rather enroll their children in a private school. If the city dwellers decide to send their children to private school — say when their children hit middle-school age — that expense would instantly make the suburbs a bargain.

While my analysis was by no means scientific, my goal was to recreate the type of decision a hypothetical family of four earning $175,000 a year might encounter. I chose an upper-middle-class income because that's generally what our family needs to earn, conservatively, to afford a median-price home in Park Slope, a section of Brooklyn that is family-friendly, has good schools and is generally more affordable than Manhattan.

This analysis breaks down some of the basic and universal expenses that an upper-middle-class, dual-income family that has a combined income of $150,000 a year would have. In both cases, I figured for two children in the family. I will show examples from the most recent calculation because, of course, it is more current and relevant.

The two-bedroom, one-bathroom co-operative apartment that we're using as the city model is listed at $675,000, close to the median price of a family-friendly, urban residential area.

We stacked that against a four-bedroom, two-and-a-half bathroom suburban sprawl that is a 30-minute commute from the city where the parents work. The house is selling for $595,000.

The result? You obviously get more space for your money in the suburbs, but it cost about $1,285 more a month, or 18 percent, including income taxes, to live there.

Specifically, each month, the suburban family needs to lay out about $5,668 to run their home and commute to work in Manhattan, compared with $3,852 for the urban family. That includes most relatively static expenses — from the mortgage, property taxes and homeowner's insurance, to transportation, utility bills and, for the house, landscaping. Even though big repairs for the house, like replacing a water heater or putting on a new roof would heap on even more costs, estimating those expenses is so arbitrary that I chose to exclude them.

A large factor that you would want to consider is really the property taxes, which can vary greatly from area to area. When I compared living in urban New York City with a suburban home in neighboring New Jersey, the New York family ended up with a tax bill that was 21%   higher that the family in New Jersey. This is because the urban family faces an additional New York City income tax and receives less of a deduction on their much lower property taxes.

The big-ticket item that pushes the Jersey costs ahead is the property taxes, about $16,000 for a house that costs as much as our $595,000 example. And then there's the cost of two cars, monthly toll passes and higher utility bills. But if you add the sky-high private school tuition to the urban family's costs — and the annual bill is often more than $25,000 a child — the pendulum would swing back in favor of the suburbs.

For wealthier families, the calculus changes again because suburban living allows them to escape New York City taxes, which, at 3.65 percent of income above $90,000, can really add up. A family making $500,000 a year will pay $15,000 in taxes to the city of New York in addition to all of the federal and state taxes they are responsible for.

Families weighing such a move need to do a fair amount of research to calculate their own monthly cash flow. The numbers will vary, sometimes greatly, depending on income, the property and state you're living in, along with a host of other factors like whether they are subject to the alternative minimum tax. Then, there is cost of home maintenance — always a wild card. Are you moving into a rambling old bungalow or a freshly renovated home?

Naturally, these decisions aren't always driven by numbers alone. Many would gladly give up the value of urban living for the space, schools, and high school football that is available outside the city. Conversely, there are still plenty of couples who are planning to raise their twins in a two-bedroom. To some, the suburbs mean boring strip malls and no diversity. They would much rather be able to walk everywhere than drive a van to soccer practice.

When You are Moving, Consider Possible Tax Deductions

Moving can often be very expensive. In many situations, Uncle Sam is willing to subsidize some of these costs. If your move is eligible, this is a great time to save some money during a time where you will probably need it most. Of course, the money you save really won't be reflected until you are filing your taxes.

To write off your relocation costs, a move must be work-related. Then you have to pass both time and distance tests. But as long as a move meets these requirements, it doesn't matter if it's your first job, the same job or a new job.

And while you have to use the long Form 1040 to claim the moving costs, you don't have to itemize any other deductions. The costs are detailed on Form 3903 and the total transferred to the adjustments to income section of your return. There is no Schedule A to complete, no percentage-of-income thresholds to meet, no deduction phase-outs because you made too much money.

The biggest moving hurdle, both practically and tax wise, is the 50-mile distance test. This stipulation is designed to ensure that your move is necessary for your job and isn't just a way to ease your daily commute to work.

Keep in mind that the 50-mile rule adds on the distance of your previous commute. The location of your new job must be at least 50 miles farther from your previous residence than your last office was. That means if you lived 10 miles from your old job, your new job must be at least 60 miles from your old home before you can deduct moving costs.

The IRS says to figure the distance using the shortest of the more commonly traveled routes; i.e., don't take the scenic route to make sure you meet the mileage measurement. Also, remember that the distance test only considers the location of your old home and how far it is from your previous job versus the one for which you relocated, not your new residence.

Then there's the time requirement. It has two components and is the IRS's way of guaranteeing that you don't use tax breaks just to help you check out the scenery around the country. First, moving expenses generally are deductible if incurred within one year of starting a new job. Secondly, you have to work full time at a new job for at least 39 weeks during the first 12 months. The worked weeks don't have to be consecutive or even with the same employer.

Self-employed workers moving to a new locale must meet the year-to-move deadline and work full time at their entrepreneurial enterprise for 78 weeks during the first 24 months. Again, the worked weeks don't have to be consecutive.

Once you meet the time and distance requirements, gather up your moving receipts. IRS-approved deductions include the costs to move household goods and personal property, limited storage and insurance fees, and utility connection or disconnection charges. Some lodging and travel expenses near your new and former homes also are deductible, as are shipping costs for your car. Uncle Sam even lets you write off the travel arrangements you make to get your household pets to your new home.

In addition to the basic eligibility and receipt requirements, here are few other things to keep in mind:
• If you're married and file jointly, only one spouse needs to meet both the time and distance tests. However, you cannot combine the weeks your spouse worked with the weeks you worked to satisfy the time-employed component.
• If your new employer reimburses you for some or all of your

transfer costs, don't look to the IRS for additional help. Moving expenses paid by your boss aren't deductible.

• If you deduct moving expenses and then don't pass the time tests, you must file an amended tax return or include the moving expenses in your income the next year.

Free Resources for Real Estate

The savings potential for this section is massive. First of all, these sites offer quality information completely free of charge. But more importantly, if you are planning a long-distance move, these resources can help you get most of the leg-work done on your computer so you can narrow down what you want before travelling out there—greatly decreasing the costs of travel. Also, if you do more of the initial work yourself, you are at more of an advantage to negotiate down the fees of a real estate agent.

Among other things, these sites allow house hunters to screen prospective neighbors, evaluate school districts and see how members of the community rate a street's Internet connectivity and cell phone service. Shoppers can keep abreast of the news in a neighborhood they're considering, and get alerts when houses list for sale or restaurants open – or when a registered sex offender moves to the area. Consumers can find energy-efficient homes and compare locations by levels of toxic waste or drought conditions. And both buyers and sellers can join discussions with others who are in the market and real-estate professionals.

You can see just about any type of information about a house on Trulia.com. For starters, users can enter a city, town or ZIP Code and see a listing of every home for sale, sortable by price, address, number of bedrooms or bathrooms, broker or type of home (single-family or multi-family). They can also narrow the search by establishing parameters for location, size and property type.

Clicking on a listing brings up a page with a more-detailed description of the home, including how long it has been on the market, and photos. This page also offers lists of similar homes for sale and similar recently sold homes, with links to pages for each of those homes; charts comparing the home's price to those of the similar homes and to the average listing and sale prices in the area; a sales history for the home, drawn from public records; and a link to a real-estate guide for the area that includes information on market trends, schools, crime statistics, income levels and commuting times.

There are also discussion boards, and users can arrange to have email alerts sent to them when properties within their search parameters are listed or sold. The site can also send alerts when the price of a particular house changes or the house is sold.

Similar features are available on Zillow.com. One feature I like is what the site calls Zestimates, which are Zillow.com's estimates of the value of homes, including homes that aren't listed for sale.

Another interesting feature of Zillow.com is that people whose homes aren't on the market but who would consider selling at the right price can post a "Make Me Move" price to see if there's any interest worth exploring.

Users of these and other real-estate sites should keep in mind that the data the sites use can sometimes be dated. For instance, information on the number of bedrooms and bathrooms may not reflect recent renovations. And the census figures the sites use for demographic profiles may be years old, so they may not reflect recent trends in rapidly changing neighborhoods or towns. Hopefully, this should change as 2010 census data filters in.

One way to supplement the statistical information on real-estate sites and to get help with particular questions or concerns is to seek input from others in the market and from real-estate professionals on the sites' discussion boards. Both Trulia and Zillow offer internal discussion where you can hammer out inquiries that the numbers just can't answer.

Other sites are designed to give users a look at neighborhoods through the eyes of the people who live there. On recently launched StreetAdvisor.com, buyers can look for input from residents of a particular street about their neighbors, local services and more.

Reviewers also rate their street for its overall "vibe," which includes neighborly spirit and night life, among other factors; for its Internet and pay-TV access and cell phone reception; for its "health," which includes factors like cleanliness, noise levels and traffic; for the cost of living and real-estate values; and for services and amenities like public transportation, medical facilities, schools, child care, and parks and recreation. Users can post pictures and videos as well.

For a different take on neighborhood life, house hunters can check RottenNeighbor.com. This site lets users post complaints about their neighbors, so it can serve as a warning about frictions in a neighborhood.

For a broad view of the environmental conditions in a neighborhood, the best resource is the Environmental Protection Agency. At EPA.gov, house hunters can click on the "Where You Live" tab to learn about levels of air and water pollution, hazardous-waste sites and releases of toxic chemicals in a given city, county or ZIP Code.

At EnergyStar.gov, a joint site of the Environmental Protection Agency and the Department of Energy, users can find builders working with the EPA to build homes that meet the government's Energy Star standards for energy efficiency. Another site, EcoBroker.com, owned by EcoBroker International, Evergreen, Colo., can also help users find homes with energy-efficient and environmentally friendly features.

Other sites specialize in information on school systems and crime statistics, areas that some real-estate agents aren't inclined to talk about because of concerns that their comments could be construed as steering people away from or toward certain neighborhoods.

GreatSchools.net offers both statically ratings of schools and feedback from actual parents of schoolchildren. The site gives information for both public and private schools, including test scores, the ethnicity of students, student-teacher ratios and spending per pupil. In addition to written reviews, parents rate schools for principal leadership, teacher quality, extracurricular activities, parent involvement, and safety and discipline. The site is owned by GreatSchools Inc., a nonprofit organization based in San Francisco. Another site, SchoolMatters.com, a service of the Standard & Poor's division of McGraw-Hill Cos., provides information on public schools only.

A Bit of Good News: Things are Getting Cheaper

Inflation, the overall general upward price movement of goods and services in an economy, is a natural process that makes us all poorer. If you have cash that you hide in a mattress, it will be worth less down the road when you take it out. The dollar amount will be the same, but you will be able to buy less with it because of rising prices. However, some trends we've seen recently regarding your home would point to falling prices. Let's take a look at how some things are getting cheaper:
Home prices, of course, skyrocketed earlier in the decade, but declines since 2007 have been taming the runaway cost of housing and making homes more affordable. Rents have been falling, too.
The price of many things inside the typical home is coming down. Furniture costs, for example, have fallen by about 12 percent since 2000, while the cost of a TV has plunged by 84 percent. Food prices have gone up, but the cost of big appliances like refrigerators and dishwashers has barely changed since 2000, which is a net improvement after inflation. And the cost of small appliances like coffee makers, toasters, and blenders has dropped by about 23 percent.
Price tags on washers and dryers are about the same as they were in 2000--which makes them cheaper, after inflation--even with snazzy new color-coordinated machines and lower energy usage. The cost of bedroom furniture has dipped by about 4 percent since 2000, while bedding, window treatments, and linens have fallen by more, thanks largely to cheap material from China and

other low-cost countries.

Computer prices have plunged by 84 percent since 2000, while Internet access, long-distance phone service, and even stationery have gotten cheaper as well.

Tools, paint, hardware, and lawn and garden equipment are about 4 percent cheaper than they were 10 years ago. Even the bench is cheaper.

The average cost of a new car is about 3 percent lower than in 2000, despite better safety equipment and more advanced electronics. Used vehicles are down even more, by about 8 percent.

So the good news is: there are deals to be found everywhere. From your office to your garage, to the house itself, there are myriad ways you can save some big money right now as a savvy shopper.

The Psychology of Saving Money

For many, saving money isn't just an action-- it becomes a way of life. It is a habit that is cultivated when we follow principles of conservation and pragmatism. Let's take a look at the ideas that can help us not just save money, but maximize our utility and live richer lives in every aspect.

Success is a State of Mind

Warren Buffett is worth $45 billion. That wealth isn't only a factor of savvy investing and good business — Mr. Buffett is also known as a penny pincher. Buffett still lives in the same Omaha, Neb., home he bought in 1958 for $31,500. Warren Buffett, among many others that are famous for their financial success, follows a few basic principles of saving money that we can all learn from.

Buy Low: As I discuss in the real estate chapter, you often make most of your money when buying something rather than selling it. The rationale here is this: If you are patient and buy things when a great opportunity for a deal rises, especially when purchasing an appreciating asset or investment, there is a much better chance that you will be financially rewarded on the sale of the item or investment.

John Paulson, a billionaire hedge fund manager, bought his summer home in the Hamptons for a steal by waiting at a foreclosure auction on a rain-soaked day. It is no wonder that Mr. Paulson has been so wildly successful as an investor because he knows that you can't lose when buying low.

Live Within Your Means (or below): I would argue that any self-made man or woman could not have become what they are today without financial discipline. You can make a lot of money, you can make a little bit of money, but the second you spend all the money is when people get into trouble. Saving is the key to preserving your wealth.

As many Americans realized during the booming real estate market, just because you think you can afford something doesn't mean you should buy it. Making sure that you are saving a sizable portion of your income and avoiding unnecessary debt will keep you financially fit, whether you become a millionaire or not.

Be Skeptical with Investment Opportunities: Ponzi schemes that have been in the news for the past few years have conned people, many of them investing elite, out of hundreds of millions of dollars. Only afterward did we learn that with a little investigation, most clients could have easily uncovered the fraud. This is easy to point out in hindsight, but it begs the question, "Didn't anybody wonder if the returns were too good to be true?"

I advise all of my clients to always be wary, because it is not just the Madoffs and con artists that will hurt you financially. More often than not, it will be a friend or family member that means well that ends up burning you in the pocket book. A prudent person must be good at saying "no."

Get Back Up and Try Again: It is easy to get discouraged in a sluggish market with high unemployment. Don't! Most successful and wealthy people have overcome obstacles and failure along the way. Steve Jobs was ousted from Apple when he was 30. Today, he's a billionaire and a legend. Plus, after getting fired, he created another billion-dollar media company, Pixar. Dusting yourself off and trying again is something all great achievers have. They have this undying belief good things will happen and will continue to happen.

Display Self-Worth: Regardless of the profession, the rich and successful tend to have a strong sense of self-worth — key to skillfully navigating an upward career path. Always put your best foot forward-- dress well, maintain a successful appearance, and show a passion for whatever work you do.

Managing Costly Expectations in the Family

The cost of raising kids is continuing to rise. A middle-income family can expect to shell out nearly a quarter of a million dollars, or $222,360, to raise a baby born in 2009 to age 18, according to the Department of Agriculture. That is up about 1.4% from 2007, before the recession began -- and it doesn't include college costs.

Now, amid tight household budgets and a growing belief that today's youth will face a lasting drop in their standard of living, many parents are working to reshape children's expectations. The result is a much needed shift in behavior, as kids learn to economize or work to pay for consumer goods they want.

The key is to resist consumer pressures. I have many clients who have had to take a more active role in helping their kids shape opinions on how money should be spent. One in particular will sit with her children while they watch TV and heckle some of the ridiculous teenage programming like MTV's Cribs and My Super Sweet Sixteen which glorify opulent spending.

In the past, money talk was taboo in many families, and many parents sheltered children from financial realities. Parents find finances one of the most difficult and stressful parts of managing families so they leave the children out to spare them the frustration. Unfortunately, this only exacerbates the financial problems of a family because the children's understanding and expectations are not in sync with those in charge of the finances-- not to mention it is depriving them of the learning opportunity that could help them down the road.

Telling a pre-teen or teen you can't afford something usually doesn't work. Kids are very concrete in their thinking. If you say at the mall, "I can't afford those shoes," then go to Costco and spend $200 on necessities, they don't understand the difference. They will just think, "There she goes again."   A better approach is to give children a budgeted amount for necessities and require them to stick to it and account for their spending.

Kids should be learning at a young age things that we

learned from experience—budgets are obnoxious but necessary, debt can be suffocating and should be avoided, and that desires need to be prioritized. The only way to teach this is to include them in the financial discussion. Talk them through monthly expenses like the utility bills and how they work—you may see an increased consciousness of energy and water usage on their part.

Peer pressure can undermine parents' efforts. While teens in the past could leave school and go home to escape, now, peer pressure never turns off. Kids go home and a friend posts a photo of her new purse on Facebook. Teens are no longer competing with the Jones's kids. They are competing with countless Facebook friends across the country.

Bucking the consumer culture isn't easy for parents either, so remember that you are setting an example with all of your purchase decisions. The good news is that the challenge of budgeting and responsible spending teaches skills and values that will be useful in all facets of life. So when you are helping to manage the spending expectations of your family, you are also giving life lessons that will pay dividends for years.

Passing on Successful Money Habits

For most adults, the first brush with money management was a piggy bank on top of their dresser. A nickel here or a dollar there for every chore completed or good deed. Financial responsibility, for the most part, stopped with the piggy bank. Many of the Echo Boomer generation—those born between the 1970s and early 1990s—agree that learning how to spend, save, and invest wisely just wasn't a part of life's lessons growing up.

Indeed, piggy banks may not be enough to impress healthy saving habits in young people. Especially these days. Many Americans are kicking themselves for being reactionary to the recent recession, scrimping and saving only after things hit rock bottom. Now faced with a deteriorating job market, fragile housing market, and the threat of a double-dip recession, more consumers are reshaping their spending habits and are showing a renewed commitment to saving—behavior we haven't seen in recent decades. The generation born during the Great Depression that went on to fight in World War II, which Tom Brokaw deemed "the greatest generation any society ever produced," had to pull itself up by its bootstraps to put food on the table. At the same time, they bequeathed to subsequent generations a life with considerable aplomb and privilege, distorting notions of what it means to work hard, survive, sacrifice, and value every dollar earned. According to a Fidelity Investments study, on average, Generation Y individuals hold more than three credit cards with one-fifth carrying a balance greater than $10,000 and 1 in 4 believing they will never be free of credit card debt during their lifetime. Parents nowadays are learning from their own mistakes, and finding themselves more mindful than ever of passing down solid financial habits to their kids.

It's clear that children today lead a more extravagant lifestyle—laden with trendy wardrobes, smart phones, video games, and other expensive gadgets—than their parents did. And it doesn't help when parents simply dole out cash with no strings attached. Upon graduating high school and flying the coop, many teenagers are likely to be walloped by exorbitant debts, making it extremely difficult to purchase a car or home down the road due to poor credit.

So, how can you teach your children the importance of saving, accounting for their spending, and self-discipline? Here are some money management strategies and tactics for parents that can help kids take control of their financial futures:

Be committed. "Like mastering a new language, developing athletic skills, or becoming a master musician, financial fluency requires time, practice, intention, the acquisition of financial language and values. This is a process, not an event, and parents who begin early find that good financial values and behavior are more deeply integrated into children's life skills and habits if they are as consistent and clear about their financial expectations as they are about brushing teeth and doing homework. Most parents understand that a couple of hours on the tennis court would not be enough to prepare a young person for competition. Similarly, a badly managed allowance and a few lectures on "spending less" are not a financial education.

Money does not grow on trees. Nor does it magically appear from ATMs. Children should learn from a very early age that they have to work to earn money. Ask them: "Do you know where money comes from?" If you go to the bank or withdraw money from an ATM, explain to your child that it is your money coming out of your bank account and that you worked for that money.

Provide a weekly allowance. Parents can pay their child a weekly allowance for completing household chores, whether it's doing the dishes, mowing the lawn, cleaning up their room, baby-sitting, or any other age-appropriate task. You can track chores or good behavior on a chart, checking off what they accomplished that day. By week's end, you can pay them for their accomplishments. Divvy up the weekly allowance into different envelopes, such as "entertainment," "clothes," or "savings."

Get a job, create a budget. Once your child turns Sweet Sixteen, require him or her to get a part-time job. The money earned can go toward things that they want, such as clothing, tech gadgets, or entertainment—but only if it falls within their budget. Your child may not have enough money to spend on an iPod because of, say, weekly transportation or car-related expenses.

Go shopping together. The supermarket is a great way to show kids how to save money. You can use the items on your list and compare prices between products, to help children look out for less-expensive brands. For the little ones, use relatable items, such as chocolate chip cookies or milk.

Start a savings account. Get your kids into the habit of saving by starting a savings account, to which they contribute a set amount each week. Set realistic goals and work with them on how they are going to achieve the goals. The account will teach them to save regularly. And reviewing monthly bank statements will help them to understand the concept of interest accrual.

Use online games and websites. A fun way to get young children interested in money management is through online games. For example, T. Rowe Price and Disney teamed up to create The Great Piggy Bank Adventure Financial Education Game, a virtual board game for children ages eight to 13 that provides education on the basics of setting goals, saving and spending wisely, and using different investment strategies for growing assets. The Kids.Gov website also offers a slew of online resources to help parents teach their kids about money.

Be healthy. I realize that eating healthy and staying in shape is easier said than done, so this is something that you and your children can work on together. If you are in good shape, you can save a lot of money on life insurance and individual health insurance plans. And as an added bonus, you'll feel better and have more energy.

Less Can Be More

Let me share the experience of a couple that were once clients of mine—we'll call them Tom and Jane. They were living in Mission Viejo, CA., making a combined $160,000 a year, and living paycheck to paycheck. Student debt was being neglected as new debt for cars, a new condo, and furniture for the new pad started to take over. They came to my office and we made a plan to curb their debt and build net worth. However, over a couple of years, this couple made more drastic changes than I typically see with people I work with.

Inspired by books and blog entries about living simply, Tom and Jane began donating some of their belongings to charity. As the months passed, out went stacks of sweaters, shoes, books, pots and pans, even the television after a trial separation during which it was relegated to a closet. Eventually, they got rid of their cars, too. Emboldened by a web site that challenges consumers to live with just 100 personal items, Jane whittled down her wardrobe and toiletries to precisely that number.

Six years after Tom and Jane began downsizing, they now live in Seattle Wa. in a one-bedroom apartment. Tom is completing a doctorate in economics; Jane happily works from home doing freelance writing and designing on the internet. They have trimmed down their belongings to very simple necessities. With Tom in his final semester of school, Jane's income of about $30,000 a year covers their bills. They are still car-free but have bikes. One other thing they no longer have: $90,000 of debt.

Jane's mother is impressed. Now the couple have money to travel and to contribute to the education funds of nieces and nephews. And because their debt is paid off, Ms. Strobel works fewer hours, giving her time to be outdoors, and to volunteer, which she does about ten hours a week for a nonprofit group.

While Tom and Jane overhauled their spending habits before the recession, millions of other consumers have since had to reconsider their own lifestyles, bringing a major shift in the nation's consumption patterns. As a nation we've become much more calculated in how we spend money out of necessity.

Amid weak job and housing markets, consumers are saving more and spending less than they have in decades, and industry professionals expect that trend to continue. Consumers saved 6.4 percent of their after-tax income in June, according to a new government report. Before the recession, the rate was 1 to 2 percent for many years. In November, consumer spending and personal incomes were essentially flat compared with October, suggesting that the American economy, as dependent as it is on shoppers opening their wallets and purses, isn't likely to rebound anytime soon.

On the bright side, the practices that consumers have adopted in response to the economic crisis ultimately could — as a raft of new research suggests — make them happier. New studies of consumption and happiness show, for instance, that people are happier when they spend money on experiences instead of material objects, when they relish what they plan to buy long before they buy it, and when they stop trying to outdo the Joneses.

If consumers end up sticking with their newfound spending habits, some tactics that retailers and marketers began deploying during the recession could become lasting business strategies. Among those strategies are proffering merchandise that makes being at home more entertaining and trying to make consumers feel special by giving them access to exclusive events and more personal customer service.

While the current increase of financial responsibility may simply be a response to the economic downturn, some analysts say consumers may also be permanently adjusting their spending based on what they've discovered about what truly makes them happy or fulfilled.

So just where does happiness reside for consumers? Scholars and researchers haven't determined whether Audi will put a bigger smile on your face than Mercedes-Benz. But they have found that our types of purchases, their size and frequency, and even the timing of the spending all affect long-term happiness.

One major finding is that spending money for an experience — concert tickets, French lessons, sushi-rolling classes, a hotel room in Monaco — produces longer-lasting satisfaction than spending money on plain old stuff. Thus, it would be more beneficial to spend your money on a vacation than on a new couch.

A recent study tried to grasp this idea by studying nine major categories of consumption. Of all of the categories, the one that had the highest correlation of increased spending and happiness was leisure: vacations, entertainment, and hobbies. So if money doesn't make you happy, maybe it is because you money isn't being spent in the right places. This research suggests that, unlike consumption of material goods, spending on leisure and services typically strengthens social bonds, which in turn helps amplify happiness.

One reason that paying for experiences gives us longer-lasting happiness is that we can reminisce about them, researchers say. That's true for even the most middling of experiences. That trip to Rome during which you waited in endless lines, broke your camera and argued with your spouse will typically be airbrushed with a much rosier recollection.

While it is unlikely that most consumers will downsize as

much as Tom and Jane, many have been, well, happily surprised by the pleasures of living a little more simply. There's been an emotional rebirth connected to acquiring things that's really come out of this recession. When I work with people that have lost a lot financially over the past few years, from everyone I hear the same thing-- that they have refocused their lives to building better relationships with family and friends.

Understanding the World of Finance

Finance is the science of money management. Personal finance includes saving money and often includes borrowing/lending money. The field of finance deals with the concepts of time, money, risk and how they are interrelated. It also deals with how money is spent and budgeted. Your mortgage, auto loans, retirement accounts, savings accounts, insurance policies, and credit are all facets of your personal finance.

Although you may find other chapters of this book more interesting or easy to understand, I promise you that this chapter will save you more money. Making educated moves and avoiding mistakes while securing one single home loan can have the same positive effect as 30 years of carefully searching coupon books before going grocery shopping. Being able to get a rate for a mortgage just 0.1% lower can equate to thousands of dollars of savings over the lifetime of the loan.

In this chapter we will go over some of these long term financial decisions we make and how you can save a great deal of money when making them. Just as importantly, we will also highlight some common mistakes that could cost you thousands of dollars in unnecessary spending.

Avoiding the Most Common Financial Pitfalls

Anyone who is honest will admit making a stupid financial decision at some point in their life. We are all imperfect and impulsive when it comes to dealing with money. Here are some common mistakes that almost anyone can relate to. Please consider these items in your lives and how to avoid them being obstacles to your own financial success:

Saving too little too late: One of the most common mistakes that people make is putting off saving their money. They see retirement as too far in the future to be pressures to step up their saving—even into their 40's. What they don't realize is that the savings may be for something even more pressing than retirement.

Unemployment, illness, injury, and natural disasters are just a few of the awful events that can occur but we rarely plan for. Not having sufficient savings in such an event can be a costly ordeal—many have to borrow money at ridiculous rates just to stay afloat in the short term while burying themselves in debt in the long term.

With the time value of money, the more you save now will mean a much larger sum down the road. Assuming that you won't have to dip into your reserves for an emergency, your savings can add up handsomely for a comfortable retirement if you are putting money away frequently in generous proportions. Commit to a saving plan now. Today. No excuses.

Paying Interest for Depreciating Assets: There are only two situations where paying interest makes sense, at least mathematically. The first is when the purchase goes up in value at a rate greater than the rate of interest you're paying to finance it. Example: You borrow money at 5 percent to finance real estate that you think might return 8 percent on your overall investment. Other examples might include a business loan or a student loan — in other words, something that's going to return more (at least potentially) than it costs in interest payments.

The other situation where paying interest makes sense is when you can earn more on your cash than you're paying in interest. Example: After taxes, I'm only paying about 3.5 percent to finance my house. Since I think can make more than 3.5 percent after-tax in the stock market, I'll forgo paying off the mortgage, even though I have the cash.

Obviously there are times when we have no choice but to borrow. The point is that unless the math works out, the less you borrow, the better.

Foregoing Free Money: If your employer is offering matching money when you participate in your company's 401k or other retirement plan — and you're not participating to the extent necessary to get the full match — you're literally refusing free money, not to mention ignoring an opportunity to get a tax deduction and grow your retirement savings tax-deferred.

There are only two kinds of people who turn down free money: people who really, truly can't afford to put up the money to get the match, and people who aren't thinking it through.

Spending More On a House than You Can Afford: You should spend no more than 25 percent of your gross income on a mortgage, regardless of what size house you really need. While spending the maximum possible amount you can afford will make real estate agents happy, will it make you happy? When you buy more square feet than you're going to actually live in, you're required to insure them, furnish them, clean them, heat them, and cool them. All of that costs money, time and stress.

Ruining Your Credit: Like many things in life, Credit is simple to screw up and awful to fix. And even though you may think it doesn't matter, some day it might, and probably will. If you've already messed up your credit, take the time and steps necessary

to fix it and then keep in good shape. Good credit will save you thousands on loans. We will discuss this more in another section.
Not Setting Goals: Whether sitting in your car or standing at the airport, you'd never start a trip without a destination in mind. The same logic applies to money. You should decide exactly what it is you'd like to accomplish, and then remind yourself of that goal early and often. Are you trying to buy a house? Become self-employed? Save for your kid's college education? Retire in your 50s? Whatever it is, write it down, picture it and share it with anyone else who you're counting on to help you accomplish it. Your goal isn't money — money is just paper. Create goals — both short-term and long-term — then decide how much money you'll need to reach them. Take it from someone who wandered aimlessly for years: goals work.
Not Budgeting Your Money: If you have a job of any kind, you can bet that your employer tracks every dime they make and every dime they spend. Granted, they have an incentive to do so — both income and expenses affect their income taxes — but it's only logical to want to know where your money is coming from and where it's going.
Tracking and categorizing your expenses with a budget is the single greatest tool you have to accomplish your money-related goals. A plan that includes what you intend to spend on things like entertainment, food, housing, etc., vs. what you actually spend allows you to fine-tune your finances and find places to save. Not doing this is like driving with your eyes half-closed: You might reach your destination, but you're certainly going to take more time getting there.

Can I Get a Mortgage Right Now?

Many of my younger clients are asking me if it is a good time to finance a home. My answer? Absolutely. In September, the national average interest rate for a 30-year, fixed-rate conforming loan (under $417,000) was 4.9%, according to

Bankrate.com, a mortgage-tracking firm. The initial rate for a 5/1 adjustable-rate mortgage (featuring a fixed rate for five years, followed by annual adjustments) was 4.2%. These are some of the best rates we've seen since the 70's.

The 30-year fixed rate for conforming jumbo loans (125% of a metro area's median home price, up to $729,750) was recently 5.0%, and for traditional jumbos, 5.7%. The conforming-jumbo program is slated to end Dec. 31, but reports say lawmakers will probably extend it as long as the housing market is in the doldrums.

So we have established that it is a good time to get a mortgage, now the question remains: Can I get a lender to give me a mortgage? Lending standards remain tight, and lenders have been picky even with the best-qualified borrowers. If you're buying or refinancing the mortgage on your primary home, you'll need a minimum down payment of 5% to 10% for a conforming loan or 10% to 15% for a conforming jumbo loan. With 20% or more down, you avoid private mortgage insurance, which typically costs 0.5% to 1.5% of your loan amount per year. Fannie Mae and Freddie Mac, which set the standards for mortgages they buy from lenders, require a minimum credit score of 620; you'll get the best rate if your score exceeds 720. The Federal Housing Administration requires a minimum credit score of 580 to qualify with a down payment of 3.5%, but FHA lenders often impose a higher minimum score of 670. (If you apply with a spouse, lenders will probably base your rate on the lower of your scores.)

Lenders will also scrutinize your ratio of debt to income. Monthly housing expenses (principal, interest, taxes, hazard insurance, private mortgage insurance and association fees) shouldn't account for more than 28% of gross monthly income. Total debt shouldn't exceed 36% of gross income, but in some cases lenders stretch the maximum to 45%. Borrowers with the strongest credit profile may push the housing ratio a bit farther.

If you're looking for the lowest rate possible, start by calling your current mortgage lender and your bank or credit union. Some mortgage brokers may be able to give you a wholesale rate that beats the rate from a bank's loan officers.

Known as correspondent lenders, they are typically large brokers that do the underwriting and immediately sell the loans they originate to wholesale lenders or investors -- meaning they can both find you a loan and approve it. If you're trying to consolidate loans, a mortgage broker may also offer more options than a retail loan officer. However, some lenders prohibit brokers from originating loans of more than $417,000.

When you're ready to get rate quotes, call your prospects in the late morning (Eastern Time), when lenders have issued the day's rate sheets but before any changes are made to them. Each lender with whom you apply must give you a good-faith estimate, and you can use the GFE to compare lenders' offerings. You don't have to pay an application fee to get a GFE, but you might have to pay about $50 for the lender to pull your credit report.

Make sure that you have already gathered the documentation that you will need. You must supply your pay stubs for the past 30 days and W-2 forms for the past two years. If you're self-employed, or if 25% or more of your income is from commissions or bonuses, you must provide two years of tax returns to offer proof of established income. Self-employed people may also need a profit-and-loss statement (if you're applying at midyear or after) so the lender can assess your company's strength.

Lenders will want to see bank, retirement-account and investment statements for the past 60 days. They'll also ask you to write letters of explanation for any red flags. For example, does your bank statement show any unusual deposits? If you're using a gift to supplement your down payment or closing costs, lenders will probably require a letter stating that the money is not a stealth loan. Does your credit history show any inquiries for new credit (which may result from mortgage shopping) within the past 90 days? If you've opened a new account, lenders will ask for a statement so they can see its terms.

If you're self-employed and your income comes up short after lenders analyze all relevant tax forms, proof of sufficient assets may overcome this dilemma, or you may have to seek nonconforming loans that banks will hold on their own books. If a lender deems your income unreliable, it may require you either to pay down debt or to close lines of credit so that you will meet the required debt-to-income ratios.

If you are only considering refinancing, you should really consider the costs if you have a fixed rate only slightly higher than current rates or an ARM that adjusted downward in the past year. Just make sure that you'll be able to recoup the cost of refinancing before you sell your home. Divide the amount of the estimated closing costs (usually 3% to 6% of the mortgage amount; look at your loan papers from last time) by the amount of the monthly savings you anticipate. That will tell you the number of months until you break even.

A second mortgage or a home-equity line of credit complicates things. If you simply want to refinance the first mortgage, your total housing debt shouldn't exceed 80% of your home's market value, or else the holders of the second lien may refuse to resubordinate (agree to stand behind the first-mortgage holder for repayment if you default).

If the holder of the second lien refuses to play ball, you could try consolidating all your housing debt into a single mortgage – so that you can use some of the loan proceeds to pay off your second lien. To get such a conforming cash-out refi, you must have at least 20% equity, and for a conforming jumbo, you need 25% to 30% equity, or 35% to 40% equity if the loan is more than $625,500. You'll also pay a higher interest rate, and paying the higher rate may not make sense. Another strategy is to take out a new home-equity line of credit from the lender of the new first mortgage and use it to pay off the old line of credit. Consider a line of credit with an option to lock in the rate.

Also, you should make sure that you are comparison shopping for any option you are looking at. Take advantage of the more consumer-friendly good-faith estimate that debuted in January. The new form makes most things clear – the type, rate and features of the loan for which you've applied, as well as the lender's cost to originate the loan and third-party fees (such as title costs and taxes) you'll owe at settlement. You can see an example if you search online for "HUD + good faith estimate."

Then use the GFEs you get from each lender to compare offerings before you formally apply for a loan. When comparing GFEs, start with the interest rate, then the lender's cost to originate the loan. If the lender offering the best rate has higher fees than other lenders, try to negotiate the fees down. In this competitive climate, you may succeed. The rates and costs on the GFE are guaranteed, and if the lender underestimates on certain charges, it – not you – must make up the difference at closing.

For home purchases, the new form doesn't allow lenders to credit your down payment, earnest-money deposit or seller-paid closing costs. So the lender may give you a supplemental worksheet showing how much cash you need to bring to closing. The costs on that worksheet aren't guaranteed. Also, regulators at the Department of Housing and Urban Development warn that some less-reputable lenders may provide a worksheet with a lowball estimate of costs prior to giving you the GFE, in hopes that you'll apply without it. Don't. Those costs aren't guaranteed, either.

Read the Fine Print

There is a new term for one of the villains of the recent foreclosure mess: Robosigners. They are employees of banks and other lending institutions that signed off on thousands of documents without reviewing them. But banks aren't the only ones speeding through the fine print of important financial documents. We as consumers are guilty of the same problem.

That cursory scan leaves many unaware of what they've committed to and – in the worst case – ends up costing them thousands more than expected. Dense contracts can include small monthly fees on a car loan, for example, totaling more than $1,200 over the life of a typical loan. Or a buried clause in a mortgage can leave a buyer on the hook for expensive repairs. And a typical sleight of hand with an adjustable rate mortgage could cost you $50,000 or more on a $300,000 loan.

It's hard to blame consumers for not pulling out the magnifying glass: Loan documents are typically long and so full of legal jargon that few people can understand what they're reading, let alone digest it quickly when a deal is on the line, consumer advocates say.

Even so, there's little consumers can do but plough through the documents. Even though it can be daunting and you may not understand all of the fine print, you are agreeing to the terms when you sign. You can always hire a lawyer to review the documents before you sign them – and in many real estate deals, it's recommended – but it's ultimately your responsibility to understand what you sign.

Here's what you need to look for and what to avoid when reviewing contracts before signing up for a life insurance policy, home mortgage, or a car loan:

A Life Insurance Policy: Unlike a car or home loan, consumers can take a few days to review a life insurance policy before signing. Take that time to look for exclusions – lest the protection end up worthless after you discover your love for extreme paddle-boarding.

The most common life insurance exclusions are certain causes of death. Suicide is almost always excluded during the first few years of the policy. And the company might not pay if the cause of death was an extreme sport, like skydiving, hang gliding or scuba diving. Some companies won't even cover you if you admit to participating in such activities. If that's the case, keep shopping: There are insurers that will cover you, albeit for a higher price. Occasional scuba diving is okay with most insurers, but regular thrill-seekers may find themselves out of luck.

This information on exclusions is listed in the terms and conditions section in the offer of coverage, which is about 10 pages long and will also be spelled out on the last form you sign. Consumers can cancel life insurance policies but will lose the money they've paid into them.

Home Mortgage: In a 10-page mortgage note, two terms are particularly important: a prepayment penalty and the margin rate on adjustable mortgages. A prepayment penalty -- a fee for paying off a mortgage early -- ranges from 1% to 3% of the total mortgage amount. That's at least an extra $3,000 on a $300,000 mortgage. If you find the clause and weren't told about it, ask to have it removed during the loan application process.

For borrowers with adjustable rate mortgages, there's a bigger issue: overly high margins for lenders. Consumers getting a 5/1 adjustable-rate mortgage -- the most common ARM -- should check how their rate will adjust after the first five years. That adjustment is based in part on the profit the lender makes when it sells your loan to an investor, called the "margin rate," and buyers can find it on the second page of their mortgage note. If the number is higher than 3%, you should consider another lender. More reasonable rates are between 2.5% and 3%, and even a one percentage-point difference could add up to more than $50,000 over the life of a $300,000 mortgage.

Closing Paperwork: Even if you wanted to pore over the 40 to 100 pages in the dozen or so documents typically signed at a real estate closing, you likely won't have the chance. The seller, attorneys and other agents aren't exactly keen on waiting patiently while you cross-reference contracts with a legal reference book. To keep it simple, look for fees that don't match original estimates, clauses that make you responsible for defects in a home and tricky tax issues if you're getting any kind of government assistance to buy your home.

To get a jump on the proceedings, ask the settlement agent -- either the title company or the attorney handling the closing -- for a copy of the closing statement, which you're entitled to 24 hours before the closing by federal law. Review all fees, including the mortgage origination, credit report and appraisal fees. If the numbers aren't the same as those quoted in the good-faith estimate you received when applied for the mortgage, insist they revert back at closing.

One item you or your lawyer will have to look for at the closing itself is a "hold harmless agreement." That clause absolves the closing agent, lending company and officer of responsibility of defects in the home, like finding Chinese drywall or mold -- in other words, it places the responsibility for any associated repairs with the buyer. If it's there, ask that it be removed. If the sale isn't a bank foreclosure, the buyer's lawyer can usually do this on the spot.

And if you're among the 10% of homebuyers who receive down-payment assistance from your state, your closing package will include details about what happens if you sell your home at a profit in the near future, typically less than 10 years. You might need to pay back at least part of the profit -- and you'll learn just how much with closer review.

A Car Loan: Car loan documents can require up to 20 signatures -- even though borrowing for a car is pretty simple. So it's easy to miss small fees and monthly payment oddities, particularly when dealers push every option before you get to the final paperwork. Look for small unnecessary fees, like an extended warranty, which costs about $20 a month, or special fabric treatments that cost about $4 per month. Dealerships will recommend these, especially if you're financing the purchase, and tout their low cost. But add those two fees to a five-year, $10,000 car loan at 5%, and they'll cost you an additional $1,200 in interest over the life of the loan.

Also, compare the promised monthly payment with what's actually in the contract. If you agreed to a "balloon payment," where you make low monthly payments for a few years, then owe a lump sum, usually of several thousand dollars, make sure both payments are in the loan documents as some dealers will try to omit the lump sum.

Getting Out of Debt

Debt is the silent financial killer. It builds up quickly even though it is discreet, but when it has built up it is hard to escape from. Some consumers are paying half of their entire income or more exclusively to interest payments. Before you reach that point, you must buck the habit and get your finances in order.

In America today, carrying some debt is unavoidable, and even desirable, for most households. But between mortgages, car payments, and credit cards, many consumers find themselves over their heads – unable to dig out from under a growing debt burden that consumes an ever growing portion of their resources.

The average U.S. household now has credit card debt of more than $9,300. Credit card companies have made running up that balance deceptively convenient. What's lost when you're on that spending spree is the realization that paying off your debt can be costly, in terms of both cash on hand and your overall financial health. Let's look at some of the steps of trimming down debt:

Assessing Your Debt: How much debt is too much? The figure varies from person to person, but in general, if more than 20% of your take-home pay goes to finance non-housing debt or if your rent or mortgage payments exceed 30% of your monthly take-home pay, you may be overextended.

Other signs of overextension include not knowing how much you owe, constantly paying the minimum balance due on credit cards (or worse, being unable to make the minimum payments), and borrowing from one lender to pay another.

If you find that you're overextended, don't panic. There are a number of steps you can follow to eliminate that debt and get yourself back on track. Working your way out of debt will, of course, require you to adjust your spending habits and perhaps be more judicious in your spending.

Start With a Budget: I know you are probably already sick of hearing me use "the B word", but it really is the first step in eliminating debt. You need to figure out where your money goes. This will enable you to see where your debt is coming from and, perhaps, help you to free up some cash to put toward debt. Track your expenses for one month by writing down what you spend. You might consider keeping your ATM withdrawal slip and writing each expense on it until the money is gone. Hang on to receipts from credit card transactions and add them to the total. At the end of the month, total up your expenses and break them down into two categories: Essential, including fixed expenses such as mortgage/rent, food, and utilities, and nonessential, including entertainment and meals out. Analyze your expenses to see where your spending can be reduced. Perhaps you can cut back on food expenses by bringing lunch to work instead of eating out each day. You might be able to reduce transportation costs by taking public transportation instead of parking your car at a pricey downtown garage. Even utility costs can be reduced by turning lights off, making fewer long-distance calls, or turning the thermostat down a few degrees in winter. There are myriad ways to reduce these costs as discussed in other chapters.

Pay off high-rate debt first: The higher your interest rate, the more you wind up paying. Begin with your highest-rate credit cards and eliminate the balance as aggressively as possible. For example, assume you have two separate $2,000 balances, one charging 20% interest, the other 8%, on which you can pay a total of 6% per month. If you were to pay 4% per month on the higher-rate card and 2% on the lower-rate card (which is typically the minimum monthly payment), you would save $961 in interest and 18 months of payments over allocating 3% to each balance.

Transfer high-rate debt to lower-rate cards. Consolidating credit card debts to a single, lower-rate card saves more than postage and paperwork. It also saves in interest costs over the life of the loan. Comparison shop for the best rates, and beware of "teaser" rates that start low, say, at 6%, then jump to much higher rates after the introductory period ends.

If you can only find a card with a low introductory rate, maximize the value of that low-interest period. By paying off your balance aggressively, you will reduce the balance more quickly than you will when the rate goes up.

You can also contact your current credit card companies to

inquire about consolidation and lower rates. Competition in the industry is fierce, and many companies are willing to lower their rates to keep their customers. Even a percentage point or two can make a difference with a sizable balance.

Borrow only for the long term: The best use of debt is to finance things that will gain in value, such as a home, an education, or big-ticket necessities, like a washing machine or a computer, which will still be around when the debt is paid off. Avoid using your credit card for concert tickets, vacation expenses, or meals out. By the time the balance is gone, you'll have paid far more than the cost of these items and have nothing but memories to show for it.

By analyzing your spending, controlling expenses, and establishing a plan, you can reduce -- and perhaps eliminate -- your debt, leaving you with more money to save today and a better outlook for your financial future.

Savings Accounts and Their Hidden Costs

Saving money is a habit that we all need to cultivate. Managing saved money well is an art. A savings account is a good thing to have to keep some of your funds secure and liquid, but not everything is rosey. You should be aware of some of the costs of having money in a savings account that you may not have considered:

Opportunity Cost: This is an economics term that means there are costs associated with foregoing another alternative. The major loss that savings account holders face is simply not getting higher returns on their money. With the largest banks currently offering around a half-percent in interest, consumers will gain greater returns in almost any other savings instrument. If your money is just going to sit there, consider placing it in a variety of mutual funds and securities. If you need the liquidity, look at online banks with higher interest rates.

While some banking institutions have rates well below 1 percent, many online institutions offer savings accounts with more than double the interest rate. Account holders also need to be aware of how their interest is compounded. Most banks compound interest daily and pay out monthly. However, a few compound much later monthly or even quarterly -- significantly reducing your returns.

Teaser Rates: The savings account with the highest interest rate may not pay off the most in the end. For example, an institution may offer a high introductory rate of 2.25 percent on their online money market accounts. However, after the first three months, the rate drops to 0.75 percent. Before signing onto a savings account, consumers should do their homework.

To combat low return rates, consumers should check out banks that offer a cash bonus for opening a savings account. With current interest rates so low, a modest $100 bonus is the equivalent of 20 years' worth of returns on a $1,000 savings account with a 0.5 percent interest rate.

Annual and Minimum Balance Fees: Some banks charge simply for the privilege of opening a savings account. For savers with low balances, a $25 annual fee and a monthly minimum-balance charge ranging from $4 to $10 can suck up your savings at an alarming rate. For consumers with low savings of $500 or less, an annual fee combined with repeated minimum balance charges can cut their savings in half in less than one year.

Withdrawal Penalties: Savings accounts are designed to provide liquidity with a few restrictions. According to the Federal Reserve, consumers can legally make six withdrawals or transfers from a savings account or money market account per month.

However, it's up to the banks to set their own rules, and many only allow two to four withdrawals without penalty. Exceed that number and you'll be hit with a withdrawal fee of $3 to $10 for each time you go over. Consumers with low account balances could also be in danger of dropping below the minimum balance and incurring extra fees.

The Perfect Credit Score

Building and maintaining good credit should be a goal of anyone looking to save money. Over the years, the sort of financial discipline required to have a good credit score will save you tens of thousands of dollars in lower interest. This is especially important for home and auto loans, but today credit scores may even be used to judge you as a candidate for a new job.

Your goal to build a high, trustworthy credit score. Although I have named this chapter "The Perfect Credit Score," I have never met anyone with a perfect, 850 credit score. According to FICO, the company that designed our current credit model, these overachievers are out there. Most people score in the middle-to-low 700s on their credit scale, but less than 1% of the U.S. population do, in fact, net a full score of 850.

In reality, you don't have to have an 850. Those with a FICO score above 760 are typically privy to most of the same benefits as those with perfect credit. Of course, a score that high isn't easy to achieve either. To reach the top tier you have to master not just the basics — maintaining positive payment history and a low debt to credit ratio, but you must pay attention to the details as well. Here are some of the traits that the higher tiers of credit-worthiness share:

Long Payment History and a Clean Record: The bulk of your credit score is determined by your payment history and the amount of debt you may or may not have currently on file. Unsurprisingly, those with perfect credit scores use credit regularly while paying it off on time, every time. They also have a squeaky clean record, which means no liens, no repossessions, and no settlements.

Diverse Forms of Credit: Credit lines fall into two major categories. Installment accounts are closed-ended and require consumers to pay a fixed amount each month until the entire balance has been depleted. These typically include mortgages or car loans.

Revolving accounts, on the other hand, limit the line of credit, but have balances that fluctuate. These essentially are the accounts tied to the credit cards in your wallet. Top credit scorers have a careful balance of both accounts on record.

Lengthy Credit Report: It is not your age that helps you build credit; it is the age of your oldest lines of credit. You should always hold onto your oldest credit cards, even if they are a charge card to a store that you no longer shop at. As long as there are no annual fees, you can only gain by keeping these older accounts open.

Limited Credit Inquiries: On the other hand, those without a store charge card shouldn't simply open one frivolously. While having large number of credit card inquires on file won't dramatically decrease your score, it can keep you from joining the credit elite, especially if several inquiries are recorded over a short period of time. Applying for credit organically as you need it is fine, but you should avoid lowering your credit score just to get a 10% discount at the mall.

Taxes, Retirement, and College

There are several points in your life where some expert advice can save you thousands of dollars. We all pay taxes every year, we all hope to retire, and any of us with children or grandchildren will contemplate the looming reality of their higher education expenses. In this chapter, we are going to cover some of the simple steps of saving on your tax bill, keeping more money when you retire, and gathering more financial aid for college.

Regarding the subject matter in this chapter, you should always consult a tax professional before making any major decisions-- the ideas in this chapter were written only to get you familiar with some options that are available.

Common Questions and Misconceptions with Taxes

Before we talk about lowering your tax bill, let's talk about some simple concepts that often come up when I meet with my clients. Remember that when it comes to saving money, a large consideration we have to consider is opportunity cost and the time value of money.

Isn't a bigger refund better? The simple answer is "no." The important line on your tax return is the "Tax Liability" line, not the "Refund or Balance Due" line. A smaller tax liability is always better. Taxpayers should plan to minimize their tax, not maximize their refund.

For example: Peter and Paul each have federal tax calculated to be $12,000 on their tax returns. Peter receives a $500 refund and Paul receives a $2,000 refund. Who made out better? Peter, with his $500 refund. They both paid the same in federal taxes, but Peter had $12,500 withheld and Paul had $14,000 taken out of his pay. Peter had use of his money throughout the year, and did not provide the government with an interest-free loan. Paul gave the government an interest-free loan of his money, while he paid for a motorcycle repair on his credit card at 17% interest.

     True, many people use their tax refund as a form of forced savings. But in this day of direct deposit, it is quite easy to set aside that extra $50 a week (or whatever your refund cushion is divided by pay periods) and have it available for that motorcycle repair, vacation or other needs. Why let the government have free use of it? Another concern might be your state's financial condition. In 2009 and again this year some states are delaying processing refunds due to their own fiscal problems.

     Many people also wonder why they are taxed on their state tax refund. This is as much a complaint as a question, since many people believe they are being taxed on this money twice. Not so. There is a good explanation for what appears to be a tax on your refund: Your state tax refund is added back in to your income and you are taxed on it, only if you itemized in a prior year and deducted that overpayment. If you deducted either state and local tax withholding or estimated tax payments on your return by itemizing on Schedule A in the previous year, you in effect deducted an amount as paid which was later returned to you as a refund. Now, you must "un-deduct" it by including the refund in income the year you receive it. That's the simple part.

     Now for the complicated part. It can get more confusing if you only received a partial benefit by deducting those taxes in the prior year. This can happen for one of two reasons. 1). Let's say your state tax refund was $1,000, but your itemized deductions were only $500 greater than the standard deduction. In that case the state tax deduction only reduced your taxable income in the previous year by $500 and only $500 of the refund belongs in income this year. 2.) If you paid the alternative minimum tax the previous year, you might not have gotten the full (or even any) benefit of the previous year's state income tax deduction. In that case, the part of the refund you must take into your income is also less than $1,000.

     That's one reason it pays, if you're using a tax professional, to bring along the previous year's return and if possible, three years of back returns.

     Many also wonder if it is wise to pay off their mortgage

faster, even though it means they are giving up a tax break on the mortgage interest reduction. There is little wisdom in having a mortgage solely for the purpose of a tax write off. For every dollar of interest you pay, you get back 25 cents (more or less depending upon your tax bracket) in a refund. You lost 75 cents. And that's assuming you itemize. If you have a small mortgage, you may do as well or almost as well claiming the standard deduction, and thus get little or no benefit from your mortgage break.

But there are other considerations when deciding on whether to maintain a mortgage or to make extra principal payments to pay it off early. Will you be "cash poor" by making extra payments, and not have funds available for other needs and emergencies? Will your employment situation be changing in some way which will make obtaining credit more difficult in the future? If so, it might be beneficial to keep the mortgage or obtain an equity line of credit now (while avoiding the temptation to tap that line without forethought.) If you must have a loan, home mortgages generally are the lowest cost option because of lower interest rates and tax deductibility.

Since there is such high interest on consumer debt, many also ask if they should tap into retirement accounts to pay off credit cards. Many people became very nervous during the recent market crash, and some emptied their retirement accounts, using the cash to pay off debts. They were scared of stocks and scared of debt, too. Even if you decide you need a more conservative asset allocation (with more bonds or cash equivalents and fewer stocks), you can do it within your individual retirement account or 401(k), without incurring the tax on retirement account withdrawals, plus a possible 10% early withdrawal penalty.

Plus, you must consider more than the tax on the withdrawal itself. The income you recognize when you withdraw cash from a traditional pre-tax retirement account can push you into a higher tax bracket, forcing more of your Social Security to be taxed or causing you to lose various tax benefits because of "phase out" rules. (Many deductions and credits are only allowed within strict income limits.)

Paying high interest rates on your credit card debt while

getting a low rate of return on your 401(k) investments seems counterintuitive, but by withdrawing money prematurely from your retirement account, you lose the chance to let your investments recover and end up having a big chunk of what you take out go to Uncle Sam. So before you decide to cash out a retirement account, ask your tax pro to calculate how much you'll owe. Plus, investigate other alternatives, including a loan from your 401(k) and withdrawals of your original contribution to a Roth IRA.

Another concern that many of my clients have is unknowingly filing their taxes incorrectly. This is a legitimate concern because tax laws are unflinchingly rigid and when you are audited by the IRS, you are pretty much guilty until proven innocent. I always ask if they have reported every bit of their income. Did you do some freelance work while you were looking for the dream job you finally landed in September? You still need to report that income in this year's return.

Some taxpayers feel that if they did not get a 1099 form then they do not have to report income received. The IRS has a long arm and seems to know what was and was not reported. To avoid this take your time and review all sources of income. What's the penalty if you don't report all income? The cost, as well as interest at 6% per year and penalties of up to 20%.

You should also avoid being lax in your definition of "business expenses" that are being written off. Business expenses need to be ordinary and necessary for the business. Taxpayers should also be able to substantiate the expenses and their business purpose if asked by the IRS or other taxing agency. If the expenses cannot be substantiated then they will be disallowed upon audit and the cost will include the tax, interest and possible penalties.

Another common mistake that is overlooked is people forget to only deduct medical expenses that are net of reimbursement. Health care expenses are a little too complex for us, so let's leave it to the experts. In IRS Publication 502, it states "You cannot include medical expenses that were paid by insurance companies or other sources. This is true whether the payments were made directly to you, to the patient, or to the provider of the medical services." You must be very careful to make sure that you are not writing off a medical expense that was really paid by your insurance rather than you.

Most importantly, you need to always keep a paper trail of it all. Receipts, receipts, receipts. I can't stress it enough. When it comes to tax time, good record-keepers will win. Charitable contributions over $200 require a letter from the charity to substantiate the deduction. Contributions in which something is received such as a dinner or merchandise can only be deducted to the extent the contribution exceeds the fair market value of goods or services received. So, if you won a pair of tickets to the Super Bowl at a blind auction for charity, but only paid $20 for them, you're out of luck (and a deduction). Then again, you do have Super Bowl tickets.

Records to substantiate a claim are just as important with vehicle mileage as well. If you use your vehicle for business, you can deduct your mileage on your tax return, but make sure you've kept adequate records. If your log isn't exact, the IRS is not going to be happy. Auto mileage needs to have a log to substantiate the amount claimed.

You should also never refuse a reimbursement from your employer for business expenses. Say your employer offers to reimburse you for the conference you attended in the spring of 2010, but you turn it down because you'd rather have the deduction. This is not a good move.

Employee-related expenses can be deducted if they are related to employment, required by the employer and not reimbursed or reimbursable. Not claiming a reimbursement from the employer if it is available does not create a tax deductable expense.

Tax Moves to Consider

At the end of every year, there are some moves that you should always consider to lessen your tax bill. As always, you should consult a tax professional to make sure any of these suggestions apply in your situation.

Increase your tax-deferred contributions: You can contribute up to $16,500 into your 401(k) in 2010; for those 50 or older, the limit is $22,000. If you're nowhere close to that amount, you can ramp up your contributions to take advantage of tax-advantaged accounts. The same goes for Roth IRAs and traditional IRAs. If you want to max out your retirement savings, now is the time to start putting more money away. (You can contribute up to the 2010 limit until April 15, 2011.)

Check out any one-time benefits that might apply: Investments in certain energy-efficient products, such as a new HVAC system, windows, or insulation, might be eligible for tax credits (for 30 percent of the cost, up to $1,500). You can check to see if you've made any eligible investments—or if you want to before the end of the year—by visiting Energysavers.gov. If you purchased your first home this year, you might be eligible for the homebuyer's credit of up to $8,000. Check the IRS website (irs.gov) to see if you might qualify and how you need to prepare. Saving and organizing all relevant paperwork is the first step.

Delay deductions: Because tax experts say tax increases are likely in the future, they recommend saving big deductions until next year, if possible. So if you're planning to make a sizable charitable contribution, for example, you might want to hold off for the sake of your tax bill. Similarly, if you have flexibility over when you receive income, you might want to get as much in the bank before December 31 so it counts as income in 2010, before any potential tax increases.

Be smart about deductions: Everyone gets a standard deduction, but that doesn't mean you should take it. Millions of people give up potential tax savings simply because they don't keep records or take the time to itemize their deductions. Especially for homeowners and those with high medical bills, missing out on itemized deductions is hazardous for your financial health. And if you do go with the standard deduction, don't just assume that you should take it on both your state and federal returns, or you could be leaving money on the table.

Think about next year: There's only so much you can do to cut your tax bill for a particular year if you wait until the last minute to prepare your return. With some advance planning, you can get a head start on next year's taxes and take the opportunity to do some things you may have missed out on in past years. Things like checking your withholding and monitoring your income can help put you in better shape next time around.

Pull out your old returns: Take a trip down memory lane to visit those ghosts of tax returns past. Your best roadmap for filing taxes accurately and efficiently lies in your own tax history. Sure, it'll bring back memories of late nights in mid-April spent frantically trying to get everything together. But without looking at your returns for past years, you won't know where to begin to look for ways to save.

Taxes for the Retired

As a retiree, managing taxes can be very complex. You not only have to consider your own tax burden, but the taxes to those that will be inheriting your estate. If you have a tax-efficient investment and distribution strategy, you will be able to keep more of your hard-earned money and enjoy the finer years in life.

Look into investments that require less or no taxes on your gains. Municipal bonds, or "munis" have long been appreciated by retirees seeking a haven from taxes and stock market volatility. In general, the interest paid on municipal bonds is exempt from federal taxes and sometimes state and local taxes as well. The higher your tax bracket, the more you may benefit from investing in munis.

Also, consider investing in tax-managed mutual funds. Managers of these funds pursue tax efficiency by employing a number of strategies. For instance, they might limit the number of times they trade investments within a fund or sell securities at a loss to offset portfolio gains. Equity index funds may also be more tax-efficient than actively managed stock funds due to a potentially lower investment turnover rate.

It's also important to review which types of securities are held in taxable versus tax-deferred accounts. Why? Because in 2003, Congress reduced the maximum federal tax rate on some dividend-producing investments and long-term capital gains to 15%. In light of these changes, many financial experts recommend keeping real estate investment trusts (REITs), high-yield bonds, and high-turnover stock mutual funds in tax-deferred accounts. Low-turnover stock funds, municipal bonds, and growth or value stocks may be more appropriate for taxable accounts.

Another major decision facing retirees is when to liquidate various types of assets. The advantage of holding on to tax-deferred investments is that they compound on a before-tax basis and therefore have greater earning potential than their taxable counterparts.

On the other hand, you'll need to consider that qualified withdrawals from tax-deferred investments are taxed at ordinary federal income tax rates of up to 35%, while distributions – in the form of capital gains or dividends -- from investments in taxable accounts are taxed at a maximum 15%. (Capital gains on investments held for less than a year are taxed at regular income tax rates.)

For this reason, it's beneficial to hold securities in taxable accounts long enough to qualify for the 15% tax rate. And, when choosing between tapping capital gains versus dividends, long-term capital gains are more attractive from an estate planning perspective because you get a step-up in basis on appreciated assets at death.

It also makes sense to take a long view with regard to tapping tax-deferred accounts. Keep in mind, however, the deadline for taking annual required minimum distributions (RMDs). The IRS mandates that you begin taking an annual RMD from traditional IRAs and employer-sponsored retirement plans after you reach age 70 1/2. The premise behind the RMD rule is simple – the longer you are expected to live, the less the IRS requires you to withdraw (and pay taxes on) each year.

RMDs are now based on a uniform table, which takes into consideration the participant's and beneficiary's lifetimes, based on the participant's age. Failure to take the RMD can result in a tax penalty equal to 50% of the required amount. TIP: If you'll be pushed into a higher tax bracket at age 70 1/2 due to the RMD rule, it may pay to begin taking withdrawals during your sixties.

Unlike traditional IRAs, Roth IRAs do not require you to begin taking distributions by age 70 1/2. In fact, you're never required to take distributions from your Roth IRA, and qualified withdrawals are tax free. For this reason, you may wish to liquidate investments in a Roth IRA after you've exhausted other sources of income. Be aware, however, that your beneficiaries will be required to take RMDs after your death.

There are various ways to make the tax payments on your assets easier for heirs to handle. Careful selection of beneficiaries of your money accounts is one example. If you do not name a beneficiary, your assets could end up in probate, and your beneficiaries could be taking distributions faster than they expected. In most cases spousal beneficiaries are ideal, because they have several options that aren't available to other beneficiaries, including the marital deduction for the federal estate tax, and the ability to transfer plan assets – in most cases – into a rollover IRA.

Also consider transferring assets into an irrevocable trust if you're close to the threshold for owing estate taxes. Assets in this type of arrangement are passed on free of estate taxes, saving heirs thousands of dollars. If you plan on moving assets from tax-deferred accounts do so before you reach age 70 1/2, when RMDs must begin.

Finally, if you have a taxable estate, you can give up to $12,000 per individual ($24,000 per married couple) each year to anyone tax free. Also, consider making gifts to children over age 14 as dividends may be taxed – or gains tapped – at much lower tax rates than those that apply to adults. TIP: Some people choose to transfer appreciated securities to custodial accounts (UTMAs and UGMAs) to help save for a grandchild's higher education expenses.

What You Should Know About Social Security

When it comes to saving money, one of the best tools that you have is planning ahead. Knowing how much to budget, how much to save, and income to expect can help you develop a strategy that will maximize your income. Social Security may be something you are planning on receiving, or you may leave it out of the equation as it may not be able to sustain itself until you reach an age where you could benefit from it. Your experience with Social Security may only be the deductions that are taken out of your paycheck. Let's look at some of the little known facts about Social Security benefits.

Just about anybody who has worked for 10 or more years is eligible for Social Security retirement benefits. You need 40 quarters (3-month period) of employment, earning a minimum income of $1,000 per quarter. The income requirement is very low, but there are some exceptions. Most federal employees hired before 1984 aren't eligible to participate. Also, railroad workers and their families generally get benefits through a separate retirement system.

The actual amount of your benefits is derived from a series of calculations. Your primary insurance amount, or PIA – the benefit you would get at full retirement age – determines the size of your monthly retirement check. According to the Social Security Administration's website, the PIA is based on the Average Indexed Monthly Earnings, or AIME, as applied to an inflation-adjusted formula. The PIA is then adjusted for whether you take retirement before or after your normal retirement age – 66 for those now reaching retirement age, but gradually adjusted to age 67 for those born after 1954 (More adjustments are soon to be made by congress because of increasing longevity in the US).

You can begin drawing reduced Social Security as early as 62. For every month you delay after reaching full retirement age, up to age 70, the monthly benefit increases. According to a recent report of the Senate Special Committee on Aging, for someone with an AIME of $5,000 in 2009, the PIA would total $1,971.

In keeping with the original intent behind Social Security -- a way to lift seniors out of poverty – lower-wage earners get a higher proportion of their earnings than higher wage earners. The maximum monthly benefit that can be received in 2010 is $2,346.

If one partner in a marriage earns significantly less than the other, the lower-earning spouse can collect spousal benefits rather than payouts based on his or her own earnings history. The spouse can get the greater of their own or 50 percent of the other spouse's PIA. The lower-earning spouse is not eligible until the higher earner starts getting benefits, but both can start as early as 62.

A divorced spouse who was married for more than 10 years and has not remarried can draw against the ex-spouse's work history. Widows and widowers can receive the higher of their own or their spouse's monthly payment, but not both. With that in mind, it is important for the higher earner to delay taking benefits for as long as possible.

But many of my clients are wondering if Social Security will even be around down the road. According to many studies, the Social Security trust fund will be able to cover its retirement and disability obligations for the next 30 years or so, after which there will be a shortfall of about 22 percent. The Senate Special Committee on Aging figures funds will fall short in 2037.

I think that some of those figures are too optimistic. The Social Security trustees assume an annual 2.8 percent inflation rate. However, historic norms are in excess of 3 percent. That's a big difference when you're talking about trillions of dollars. We could make small adjustments now and bring it to fully fundable status; if we delay, it will be more painful. In 10 years the shortfall will be significantly bigger; in 20 years it will be through the roof.

Lastly, I am often asked what happens to the money that

is taken out of my clients' paychecks by the IRS. In theory, they're held in trust by the government. But it's not as if your money sits there in the Social Security trust fund waiting for you to retire. After current beneficiaries are paid, surplus dollars are used to buy bonds from the U.S. Treasury. So the trust has the bonds, but the money is now in the Treasury, where Congress can use it for any purpose. This trust is basically an account full of IOUs from the government, and to be honest, it is not an effective way of protecting your funds that you've contributed from inflation.

      2010 is the first year that Social Security has had to cash in one of those bonds in order to meet its payroll. This is a function of the demographics of our labor force. Right now, there are not enough funds generated from current workers to support the increasing number of individuals applying for benefits. From this point forward, an increasing number of those bonds will have to be pulled out every year – and Congress is going to have to find a way to come up with all that money.

Financial Aid for College

      Many people are trying to find ways to save money so that they can put funds away for their children's education. But when the day comes to actually pay, you would be wise to find every outlet you can to lower the costs of tuition and other fees. Most universities have a financial aid office with qualified people that can help you maximize the resources available to you. Unfortunately, the current economic state has left many such programs strapped for cash.

      Faced with steep budget cuts and slumping endowments, universities around the country are raising tuition and paring back aid, putting additional strain on families supporting college students. Even state schools, which are traditionally more affordable than private schools, are severely ramping up the costs for students—some as much as 32% for tuition costs. Many schools are replacing grants given to students with loans instead.

With the costs of higher education markedly outpacing the rate of inflation, future college costs are on the mind of virtually every parent of young children today.

Fortunately, there are a surprising number of short- and long-term strategies that parents can use put their finances in the right light to qualify for more aid and save thousands of dollars.

While working with a school, keep in mind that your current financial situation isn't necessarily the be-all and end-all. If your financial circumstances have changed materially at any time, ask the aid office to review your aid package. Under a "professional judgment review," financial-aid officers can make adjustments to the aid package if there have been material changes to the family's income or assets.

Schools say they are seeing a rise in the number of students asking for help. Financial-aid applications at the University of Michigan, for example, are up 4% for the upcoming academic year, on top of a 15% increase last year, and the school is making more adjustments to student aid packages to account for factors such as job losses.

Families with kids attending private colleges may be able to qualify for help under the College Board's CSS/Financial Aid Profile, which is used to determine how to distribute the school's own funds. The CSS/Profile weighs factors, such as home values, that the Free Application for Federal Student Aid, or FAFSA – which is used to determine a family's eligibility for federal grants and loans – doesn't consider. Has your home declined in value? If so, think about getting a market appraisal or a 30-day "quick sale value" to document the loss. In addition to home equity, many private schools' formulas also factor in private school tuition for younger siblings and medical expenses. If you can document that the value of your home has decreased by 20% to 50%, it has the potential to make a difference of a few thousand dollars.

For financial-aid purposes, the most crucial year is the one that begins on Jan. 1 while your child is a junior in high school – the "base income year." During that time, and throughout college, income earned or received is counted more heavily than assets in the financial-aid formulas. Try to avoid taking retirement distributions or realizing large capital gains during that period. Load up on contributions to retirement plans before the base and college years, because assets in those accounts aren't counted in the aid formulas.

Some families may want to defer converting an IRA to a Roth IRA, even though new laws now make it possible for wealthier taxpayers to take advantage of the conversion. Many financial-aid offices may use the income generated from the conversion to reduce the students' eligibility for need-based aid — unless parents appeal the offer through professional judgment.

Since financial-aid forms ask parents to list the funds in their accounts the day they fill out the forms, aim to draw down those accounts as much possible before filing out the paperwork. If you were already planning to make a big purchase — say, a new car or computer — just buy it sooner.

Spend down assets in the student's name first, since aid formulas count student assets more heavily than parental assets. Custodial accounts, such as UTMAs and UGMAs, can also be liquidated with the proceeds transferred into a custodial 529 plan, which are currently counted as a parent asset on the FAFSA form.

Some families may want to consider margin loans, passbook loans (which use savings accounts as collateral) or a home-equity loan to help pay for college since such loans reduce net assets in the aid formula. If, for example, you have a $20,000 stock portfolio and a $5,000 margin loan and have no other investments to report, you'd report $15,000 as the figure for your assets on the FAFSA. A major drawback: If the stock market declines drastically, you may be asked to put up additional stock as collateral or pay back part of the margin loan.

Another strategy: Use one of the more than two dozen "prepaid" 529 plans, which allow families to make an upfront payment in exchange for future tuition contracts or credits. The tuition guarantees generally apply to state schools in the state where they are offered, though you can use the money to help pay for out-of-state or private schools. Although many prepaid plans are operating in the red, for now they are still paying tuition as agreed. But the fine print in some state contracts gives them some wiggle room to pay out less than the promised amounts, so read it carefully.

Automobile Expenses

Cars have always been a gray area for me. I have always tried to be as pragmatic and responsible in spending money all of my life. After all, your car can be a huge drag on your bottom line. Cars themselves are expensive, maintaining them is expensive, insuring them is expensive, even parking them can get expensive (just ask my brother that pays $700/month in Manhattan just for a parking space). Yet, I love them. I have always been a sucker for sports cars.

If everything was only dollars and cents, this chapter would be short. I would advise you to get a Toyota Yaris or Honda fit. They are both cheap, cheap to maintain, and get great mileage. The expenses associated with either of these vehicles for one year are almost half the expense of the average car on the road today. But not everyone wants to drive a Yaris or Fit. I have friends that will never buy anything but a truck, even if they rarely use the truck bed for anything.

The purpose of this chapter is not to get you to change your style. Buy a car that suits you. The purpose here is to help you to save money regardless of the vehicle that you choose to buy. We will discuss a few of the easiest ways to save money on buying cars, insuring cars, and fueling cars.

Buying a Car

Buying a car is one of life's biggest expenses, but there are plenty of ways to save money, and the benefits add up fast.

Unless your job or your professional image depends on having swanky wheels, discipline yourself to separate your emotions from your buying decision. Don't buy fancy, and don't buy new.

You can save at least $9,000 in the first five years after buying a used car instead of a comparable new one, according to car-buying site Edmunds.com. The longer you keep your car, the more you save money.

Your best ammunition when you're car shopping is information. The more you know about the type of car you want and how much you're willing to pay, the stronger your bargaining position.

Most of that research can be done from your desk. The auto section of Bankrate.com has calculators and insurance information to help you with different payment scenarios. Consumer Reports offers details on most makes and models, including how much the dealer paid for the car — a key fact for the consumer.

The federal government also has several sites that can help you hone your decision and save money. One website, Fueleconomy.gov, gives you the lowdown on gas guzzlers versus fuel sippers while Safercar.gov has safety ratings, recall alerts, and crash and rollover tests.

Print out the research, make a folder and take it with you to the dealerships. The more you know the more money you'll save. And be sure to get any offers they make in writing.

When you're buying a car, don't be lured by slick ads. Set up a shopping schedule that includes visits to several dealerships, and stick to it even if you've found your dream car on the first lot. If you stay true to your schedule, you won't be tempted with an impulse buy. And let the salespeople know you're shopping around.

Schedule your dealer visits during the week rather than on weekends. You want to have the undivided attention of the salesperson when you start to negotiate prices. You can find bargains at the end of the month, when sellers are more anxious to make their quota. But be prepared for more aggressive tactics from salespeople hustling to make their numbers.

You can also shop for cars online, but don't forget about newspaper ads from individual sellers or the "For Sale" sign on the car in your neighbor's driveway.

Buying a car with cash is the optimal situation in my opinion. You should always avoid financing an item that depreciates in value—a car, for example. Buying a car in cash will also help you to be more realistic when it comes to buying a car that you can actually afford. Buying cash also takes away an area where car dealers can rip you off.

If you need to finance, know your credit score, research interest rates online and shop around at banks and credit unions for a low-interest car loan before stepping into a dealer showroom. If you go in as a cash buyer or with your own car loan already approved, you can avoid the dealer's finance office. Doing so can shave several thousand dollars off the cost of your car.

Car Insurance

The cost of insuring a vehicle can take a big bite out of your budget each year. The average consumer ends up paying around $1400 a year in insurance and could be paying hundreds less if they followed a few simple tips.

You should drop coverage you don't need. The beauty of doing a car insurance coverage checkup every six months or so is that even if it turns out that your current car insurance coverage is still the best value out on the market you may just find out that you are paying for a part of your auto insurance policy that you no longer need.

Not only do insurance rates change quite often but your insurance needs change more often than you may think. If you have a new teenage driver or have added a new car to your policy or have moved to a new zip code or—well, the list goes on and on. All of these things may potentially cause you to be paying for coverage that you no longer need.

Never assume that because you searched for all of the car

insurance discounts available 6 months ago that now there are no new discounts that you may be eligible for. New opportunities for saving money with a car insurance discount program pop up all of the time as different companies announce different discount programs in order to increase their market share.

      It's no secret that a better credit score will result in better car insurance rates. You may have been working hard to improve your credit score over the last few months in order to qualify for lower interest rates for a home loan or auto loan and you are now starting to see some of your hard work pay off.

      When you see an increase in your credit score don't let the opportunity slip by to check and see if this credit score improvement will result in an improvement in your auto insurance rates as well. You've worked hard to improve your credit score so why not spend a few minutes to see if that can only help you get a lower interest rate but a lower car insurance rate as well?

      Here is another way that you can shave off 1 percent to 5 percent off of your total car insurance premiums: Start paying your premiums with your rewards card. With the average cash back credit card earning you anywhere from 1 percent to 5 percent cash back that's like getting a bill from your insurance company and then having to only pay 95 percent to 99 percent of the total instead of the full 100 percent!

      One to 5 percent may not seem like much but as you can see with a cash back credit card calculator that money can quickly start to add up--depending upon how much money you spend each month if you use that cash back card for many of your purchases then your savings could end up being enough to pay for an entire year of college tuition after 15 to 20 years!

      Most insurance companies offer discounts to customers who are willing to pay for their policies in one or two lump sums over a year. Spreading your payments out month to month may seem less expensive than spending hundreds of dollars once a year, but the policy price is generally higher when it is spread out over twelve months. Even paying for your policy every six months is less expensive than paying for it every single month. Talk to your agent about the fees that are attached with a monthly payment so that you will be aware of the savings involved in paying annually or semi-annually.

Virtually all of the major car insurance companies offer some form of good student discount. If your kids get good grades then you save money. Some companies offer savings for a lackluster C while most offer savings for you that range from 5 percent to 15 percent if your student maintains a B or an A on their report cards.

There are also driving courses available for your children or yourself that could reduce the cost of your premium. Check with your car insurance company as to what type of courses and course providers they will recognize for a discount on your policy.

Did you know that when car insurance actuaries calculate car insurance rates that they actually assign different risk classes to different types of occupations? Some occupations have cheap car insurance rates while other occupations get assigned an added level of risk that increases their rates. The various occupation risk assessment algorithms will vary from one insurance company to the next but generally speaking professions like engineering and teaching will receive lower car insurance rates than business owners and attorneys. So what do you call yourself if you are an engineer that owns their own business? I would call myself an engineer when working with my insurance company.

If you ever are in a situation where you need to file a claim and cash in on your vehicle insurance, you should be familiar with what your policy covers. Did you know that all the personal possessions you carry in your vehicle are not covered under your car insurance policy? That's right, even the most comprehensive car insurance policy will not reimburse you for items that are stolen or damaged while in your car. You will be compensated for any damage that is done to your vehicle, but your possessions are not considered part of the vehicle's value. The best idea is to refrain from carrying extremely valuable items with you when you are driving.

However, if you are like most people in today's age, your cell phone, laptop, and GPS unit are considered essentials. The trauma of losing these items is bad enough. In today's economy, chances are the average person does not have the money on hand to run out and purchase new ones. Therefore, it is important to make sure you have your items insured. In order to insure the items you carry with you, it is necessary to purchase a rider on your home insurance policy. Always keep receipts and make sure you have photos or video of your items to prove their condition before they were damaged or stolen.

When you purchase a vehicle today, it has become standard to receive a car history report. That's great for the buyer, but not so great for the seller if your vehicle was in an accident and you never received compensation for the diminished value of your vehicle. When you go to trade your vehicle in you will not receive as much for it. Even if your car was repaired by a good quality auto body shop, the resale value will be reduced simply because it was in a collision. Most buyers will not purchase a vehicle that has been in an accident unless they receive a discounted price. Your insurance company must reimburse you for your damages. They will not automatically send you a check for your diminished value. You must file this claim in addition to your regular claim and prove your vehicle has received a loss in value due to the accident.

This is a lot easier to do on a newer car but not impossible to do on an older car. Diminished value claims are generally offered to the person who received damage from the insurance company of the person who is found at fault in the accident. Insurance companies rarely offer diminished value payments when they are reimbursing the primary driver insured on the policy.

The tax and registration fees on your vehicle may be covered by your insurance company if your vehicle is declared a total loss. In some states, the car insurance company must pay for the taxes and fees up front and in other states, the insurance company provides reimbursement after the settlement. Some states only require the insurance company to reimburse you for the tax and registration if a new vehicle is purchased within a specific amount of time after an accident. If you are being reimbursed by the other party's insurance company, they might not be required to pay you for the cost of tax and registration.

The bottom line is that you should read your car insurance policy thoroughly so that you are aware of the things that are covered and the things that are not. Many minor details can make a huge difference when you need to file a claim after a collision. For example, if you loan your car to a friend and he or she is involved in an accident, your car insurance will pay for the damages regardless of your friend's insurance situation. Little things like that can increase your insurance costs, which means you should be aware of them when you purchase a new policy.

Saving on Every Day Vehicle Expenses

If you're following the frugal path and are about to buy a used car, take it to a trustworthy mechanic before you close the deal. If you don't have a good mechanic, find one. Seek out word-of-mouth recommendations from friends with well-maintained cars.

Treat your relationship with your mechanic like you would with your doctor. This is the person who will help prevent expensive disasters if you pay him or her regular visits and follow his or her advice. If you maintain your car, you're avoiding expensive repairs down the road.

It's far cheaper to change a few hoses than to replace a blown engine. So, take the time to get your car serviced regularly and save money in the long run. And if you bought from a dealer, take full advantage of the warranty and follow the recommended maintenance schedule.

Also, you should use all the resources available to use your vehicle more efficiently. Smart-phone applications help you find everything from the cheapest gasoline in town to a map of the most efficient route to your office. I like to use GasBuddy.com which helps you to find the lowest gas rates in your area, or en-route on a trip. If you are taking a trip, you can also use Fuelcostcalculator.com to correctly budget how much money you will spend on gas for a trip.

Many businesses and schools facilitate car pooling. If your company doesn't yet, start one. You can even save money on tolls and time on some highways that give breaks to high-occupancy vehicles. When you're car pooling, you're saving money on gas, on tolls and on maintenance. You can use the high-occupancy vehicle lanes, so you get to work faster.

Even simple things like parking in the shade during the summer can help you save money. You'll work your car's air conditioner less and it will maintain your vehicle's paint job longer.

Technology and Saving Money

Like it or not, technology is the largest catalyst of growth in the world economy. The recent trends of increased connectedness, being able to work and email from your cell phone, and social media are just the beginning. The constant improvement in technology has been a huge benefit as a whole, but it has also become an enormous expense to the consumer. Computers, cell phones, and other electronics that are incredibly expensive can become outdated in as little as 18 months.

On the other hand, many recent advances have been made to save consumers great deals of money. Shopping over the internet has increased availability of hard-to-find items and drastically reduced prices. Consumer research is simpler and new apps and programs are made every day that can save you money as well as simplify your life.

In this chapter we will look at both sides of the coin. We will talk about saving money on the new largest expense for families after their car: computer expenses. We will also be looking at resources, most of them free, available on the internet that can help you save your hard-earned money.

How to Save on Computers

According to the Consumer Electronics Association, the average computer costs $550. But even if you need a high performance machine, there are still ways that you can lower that price. Let's look at some ways you can keep your costs down while still getting a great product:

Pick up a refurbished machine: Computer makers, including Apple, offload these items for highly discounted prices—often about 25 percent off—on their websites. Like new models, these products usually carry a warranty, and they go through strict quality control, too. Many of the items never had any problem to begin with-- they were returned and re-packaged. This can give you a large discount and a product that is no different than a brand-new retail machine.

Don't be brand loyal: Most machines are similar to one another in terms of quality, including brands that you might not be familiar with, such as Asus and Acer, which can sell for hundreds of dollars less than leading names. Most computer makers buy components from the same places, which essentially will only make their machines different in branding.

Skip the extended warranty (usually): If a desktop is going to break, it will probably do so within the manufacturer's warranty period. A laptop, however, is more fragile and often requires repairs later in its life, so a warranty good for three more years can save you money down the line. But don't buy it from a store or the manufacturer; get it from an independent provider, like Squaretrade.com. For example, you'll pay $130 at a retailer, but only $50 online. And consider getting a warranty with accident coverage. You'll pay 50 percent more for this protection, but you'll be covered if you drop your laptop.

Don't buy more memory than you need: The minimum amount of RAM that comes with most computers is enough to handle basic tasks, such as e-mailing photographs and watching a video, says Barrett. If you need to perform more advanced functions, such as video editing, find out how much more memory you will need (the software should say how much is required), then upgrade at a lower cost (typically $50 to $200) after you buy your computer.

Online Resources That Will Save You Money

Below I have listed some sites that are used by my clients for research and purchases. You would be surprised how much money can be saved by habitually using these tools to inform your spending.

Retailmenot.com: This site amasses coupon codes for discounts at 15,000 online merchants. After you enter the e-tailer's Web address, you will get a code to receive your price break. Go mobile with cellfire.com, a site that lets you access coupons on your cell phone. Then you show the code on your tiny screen when you are at checkout.

Beatthat.com: We all know someone who is passionate about tracking down the very best deals. With BeatThat, an entire community of such people is put to work for you. Those who find the very best deals are put into a daily drawing that can earn them $50 to $125. With an incentive like that, topnotch results are guaranteed – and spammy, unreliable "deals" are kept out of the loop. The site once focused strictly on electronics; today, you can find deals on just about anything that can be purchased online.

Gasbuddy.com and gaspricewatch.com: These track the cheapest gas stations by area. Plug in your destination to find the best places for filling up. All of the prices are kept up to date by customers like you.

Smartypig.com: These days, brick-and-mortar banks aren't offering very competitive interest rates for savings accounts. SmartyPig allows you to create a virtual piggy bank, set up savings goals and solicit donations from friends and family – all while enjoying a practically unheard-of interest rate. Once you achieve your goal, the savings – plus any interest – can be added to a debit card, sent to your bank account or added to a retail card.

Shopittome.com: Have you ever stumbled upon an amazing sale on your favorite designer clothing brand, only to discover that they are out of your particular size? At times like those, the urge to have your very own personal shopper couldn't be stronger; Shop It To Me is the next best thing. Simply plug in the sizes you wear and the designers you love, and the site will alert you to incredible deals from across the web. You can be alerted as frequently, or infrequently, as you'd like – and you'll always stay abreast of the lowest prices on the clothes you adore.

Zilok.com: If the thought of buying a new chainsaw for a one-off project makes you cringe, relax – Zilok is a site that lets you rent everyday items from everyday people in your area. Better still, you can list items that you'd happily let others rent in order to make a little extra money. The entire process is regulated through the site, ensuring that everything goes smoothly. It's a smart way to avoid buying big-ticket items that you don't need on a regular basis.

PriceGrabber.com: This is known as the granddaddy of the comparison-shopping sites: It searches millions of products — groceries, computer software, you name it — from hundreds of vendors to get you the best price.

Billshrink.com: Who doesn't want to save money on credit card fees? Now you can get a list of credit card offers, cell phone plans, cable packages, and savings account offers that are better than what you have in less than 5 minutes. Answer a few questions about your current plan and BillShrink will recommend better options to fit your needs.

Priceprotectr.com: A tool that helps you get money back if items you bought have dropped in price. Register your purchases, and e-mails will arrive when the prices have fallen. Claim the cash with an e-mail, phone call, or store visit.

Couponsherpa.com: The days of waiting for the weekend circulars to arrive in order to find the best coupons are long gone. Thanks to the Internet, there are more options for tracking down deals and savings than ever. The major caveat here, though, is sorting through all of the offers that turn up in any given search. Coupon Sherpa compiles user-submitted online coupons, printable coupons, grocery coupons and even mobile coupons and ranks them according to how many votes they receive. With a few clicks of the mouse button, you'll be on your way to exceptional savings!

Freecycle.net: During tough economic times, donating used items – and using donated items – makes all kinds of sense. On Freecycle, you can find your local group and peruse listings of free, unwanted things. On the flip-side, you can post free ads for things that you'd like to give away. This especially comes in handy when you have extra items left over from a garage sale. There's even a mobile app available that allows you to keep an eye on new listings while on the go.

Thegrocerygame.com: For a fee (cost: $10 for two months) this site provides a weekly list of the lowest-priced products at your favorite supermarket, matched up with manufacturers' coupons and specials to save even more. You can pay extra to sign up for multiple grocery stores.

Smarthippo.com: Navigating the tumultuous waters of mortgages, banks, lenders and loan officers can make even the most levelheaded person positively seasick. Instead of picking up the phone and subjecting yourself to one spiel after another, why not pick the brains of those who have been there and done that? At Smart Hippo, regular people post reviews of their experiences with all sorts of mortgage-related products and services. The stress and aggravation of buying a new home can be slashed by frequenting this simple-to-use website.

Honesty.com: This tool lets you know how much things usually go for on eBay and what's currently for sale there, so you don't overpay when you buy. Type in an item name for price comparisons on current and recent eBay listings.

Bookingbuddy.com: This site consolidates many travel sites to get you low airfares, hotels, car rentals, and vacation packages with a targeted search. Enter details of your trip once, and then click on the names of the Websites you want Bookingbuddy to search — from Expedia to Priceline.

Mylifescoop.com: Do you have a closet full of gadgets you don't understand how to use? If you like cool toys but hate reading manuals, then MyLifeScoop is the community for you. This site offers thousands of surprising ways to make use of everyday technology. (For example, do you know which smartphone apps can protect your family in an emergency?) Written in plain English, the tips from MyLifeScoop can help anyone get the most out of their tech purchases.

Pricespider.com and wishradar.com: These sites hunt online for the items you want at the most you're willing to pay. Create a wish list and the most you'd spend for each purchase. Then the sites search for the products, e-mailing you when they turn up your desired price — or less.

Couponmom.com: Use this website to locate grocery coupons, grocery deals by state, online coupon codes and so much more neat stuff to save on. Treat yourself and your family to a nice meal and save yourself money when you present the restaurant coupon that you found on 'The Coupon Mom'.

Crossloop.com: Is your child a whiz at solving computer problems, but attends school thousands of miles away? Thanks to CrossLoop, you don't have to say goodbye to their assistance when they fly the coop. The site allows users to link their computers remotely, making it possible for one person to solve another's computer issues from anywhere in the world. Various levels of service are available; if you're a computer whiz, you could even make some extra money by signing up for a pro account and setting up a profile.

Streetprices.com: This site charts price changes for popular items over time to help you determine if now is a good time to buy that new flat-screen TV. With one click you can check eBay or Craigslist as well as online retailers.

Covestor.com: We'd all like to get ready for retirement with smart investments. But who has the time to keep track of stocks on a daily basis? Covestor is a site that lets you ride on the coattails of savvy investors who share their portfolios with the unwashed masses. The site is easy to navigate, with intuitive search options and useful rankings. Best of all, users have the option of automatically matching the trades that are made by the investors that they like the best.

Upromise.com: Your kids may be babies or toddlers right now; before you know it, though, they'll be striding across the stage accepting their high school diplomas. Will you have enough money saved up to send them to college? Upromise partners up with thousands of retailers who contribute anywhere from 1% to 25% of your purchases into a college savings account. When the time comes, that money can be put into a 529, used to pay for college expenses or used to pay down student loans. It's totally free and it couldn't be easier.

7555540R0

Made in the USA
Lexington, KY
30 November 2010